Battlegroun

LADYS___TH
The Siege

Other guides in the Battleground Europe Series:

Walking the Salient *by* Paul Reed
Ypres - Sanctuary Wood and Hooge *by* Nigel Cave
Ypres - Hill 60 *by* Nigel Cave
Ypres - Messines Ridge *by* Peter Oldham

Walking the Somme *by* Paul Reed
Somme - Gommecourt *by* Nigel Cave
Somme - Serre *by* Jack Horsfall & Nigel Cave
Somme - Beaumont Hamel *by* Nigel Cave
Somme - Thiepval *by* Michael Stedman
Somme - La Boisselle *by* Michael Stedman
Somme - Fricourt *by* Michael Stedman
Somme - Carnoy-Montauban *by* Graham Maddocks
Somme - Pozieres *by* Graham Keech
Somme - Courcelette *by* Paul Reed
Somme - Boom Ravine *by* Trevor Pidgeon

Arras - Vimy Ridge *by* Nigel Cave
Arras - Bullecourt *by* Graham Keech

Hindenburg Line *by* Peter Oldham
Epehy *by* Bill Mitchinson
Riqueval *by* Bill Mitchinson

Boer War - The Relief of Ladysmith, Colenso, Spion Kop *by* Lewis Childs

Accrington Pals Trail *by* WilliamTurner

Poets at War: Wilfred Owen *by* Helen McPhail and Philip Guest

Gallipoli *by* Nigel Steel

Battleground Europe Series guides in preparation:

Ypres - Polygon Wood *by* Nigel Cave
La Basseé - Givenchy *by* Michael Orr
La Basseé - Neuve Chapelle 1915 *by* Geoff Bridger
Walking Arras *by* Paul Reed
Arras - Monchy le Preux *by* Colin Fox
Somme - Following the Ancre *by* Michael Stedman
Somme - High Wood *by* Terry Carter
Somme - Advance to Victory 1918 *by* Michael Stedman
Somme - Ginchy *by* Michael Stedman
Somme - Combles *by* Paul Reed
Somme - Beaucourt *by* Michael Renshaw

Walking Verdun *by* Paul Reed

Poets at War: Edmund Blunden *by* Helen McPhail and Philip Guest

Isandhlwana *by* Ian Knight and Ian Castle
Rorkes Drift *by* Ian Knight and Ian Castle

With the continued expansion of the Battleground series a Battleground Europe Club has been formed to benefit the reader. The purpose of the Club is to keep members informed of new titles and key developments by way of a quarterly newsletter, and to offer many other reader-benefits. Membership is free and by registering an interest you can help us predict print runs and thus maintain prices at their present levels. Please call the office 01226 734555, or send your name and address along with a request for more information to:

Battleground Europe Club
Pen & Sword Books Ltd, 47 Church Street, Barnsley, South Yorkshire S70 2AS

Battleground South Africa

LADYSMITH
The Siege

Lewis Childs

Series editor
Nigel Cave

LEO COOPER

First published in 1999 by
LEO COOPER
an imprint of
Pen & Sword Books Limited
47 Church Street, Barnsley, South Yorkshire S70 2AS

ISBN 0 85052 653 1

A CIP catalogue of this book is available
from the British Library

Printed by Redwood Books Limited
Trowbridge, Wiltshire

*For up-to-date information on other titles produced under the Leo Cooper imprint,
please telephone or write to:*
Pen & Sword Books Ltd, FREEPOST, 47 Church Street
Barnsley, South Yorkshire S70 2AS
Telephone 01226 734222

Front cover illustration: In Rotterdam, at the time of the South African War, there was a theatre called the 'Transvalia'. The walls of the foyer were ornamented by representations of battles of the conflict, and were mainly favourable to the Boers. They were executed on 150mm square tiles but eventually were papered over and lost until the place was restored in the 1960s. They now adorn the walls of the War Museum of the Boer Republics, Bloemfontein and, by kind permission, our front cover is 'Ladysmith' from that series.

CONTENTS

Introduction by Series Editor...6
Acknowledgements...8
Advice for Tourers...9

Chapter 1 **Background**...10
Chapter 2 **Talana Hill 20 October 1899**...31
Chapter 3 **Elandslaagte 21 October 1899**..51
Chapter 4 **Ladysmith under Siege**..70
Chapter 5 **Platrand 5/6 Jan 1900**...107
Chapte 6 **After Platrand, and afterwards still**.................................126

Selective Index 141

The mules' stampede at Nicholson's Nek which resulted in the surrender of 954 British Soldiers.

Introduction by Series Editor

This book is the companion of Lewis Childs' earlier work, *Ladysmith: Colenso/Spion Kop/Hlangwane/Tugela,* and completes the story of the events in that town for the four months during which it was besieged (November 1899–February 1900) and the engagements leading up to the siege.

The Boer War was of great significance in the evolution of the British Army, leading to considerable reforms. It had a great impact on those who served in it, many of whom (amongst the officers) went on to hold high rank in the cataclysm that was the Great War. It provided the British army with far more campaigning experience than their allies and protagonists on the Western Front, and important lessons were learnt (and many were not as well!). Notable amongst these was the change that was brought to the cavalry, uniquely amongst the European powers trained to operate as mounted infantry.

It was also of significance to the foreign policy of Great Britain; an imperial power which had attempted to remain aloof from the squabbles on the continent, she found herself facing serious problems in adhering to a policy of 'glorious isolation'. Sentiment was anti-British and pro-Boer and, although this was not the only cause, or even the most important, British policy after the war was to engage in a series of more or less binding agreements with other powers so that she would not be left in this unhappy situation again. A review of policy led to the conclusion that there would never be a war against the United States, and so garrisons and naval forces in that part of the world were drastically curtailed; agreements with Japan reduced the Far East commitment of the Fleet; an understanding with the French reduced the military and naval force in the Mediterranean and even the threat to India from Russia was diminished by an extension to that power of the *Entente Cordiale*.

This evolution did not happen overnight, but a decade or so after the guns fell silent in South Africa both British policy and her army had been galvanised into dramatic change.

Lewis Childs provides a contextual narrative to the outbreak of hostilities; this is important as it is complex – far more so, in many respects, than the series of events that led to the outbreak of the First World War. Tucked away in local county record offices and regimental museums are numerous accounts by soldiers who fought in the difficult circumstances of country and climate. For rather too long these have been ignored, overshadowed by the far greater conflict that broke out only a few years after the South African war was resolved. He uses these records to great advantage, adding a depth to the dusty, often rather neglected, memorials that remain as a physical reminder of the fighting. He then leads both the visitor – and, by the use of some excellent photography – the reader who is unable to be there, through the stunning South African countryside, to put the battles, engagements and incidents in the context of the ground today. He does this with both a sound grasp of the war and of Natal, a combination that well serves the memory of those who were engaged in that conflict of a century or so ago.

Nigel Cave
Ely Place, London

Maps

Cape to Cairo Railway **page 18**
South Africa 1899 **page 19**
Approach to Talana Hill **page 34**
Talana Hill **page 47**
Approach to Elandslaagte **page 52**
Elandslaagte **page 56**
Ladysmith Area **page 82**
Platrand **page 108**

Acknowledgements

At the start of *Ladysmith: Colenso, Spion Kop, Tugela* I acknowledged the co-operation given to me by people with information on the Boer War, and I am still surprised and delighted by the response of Regimental Museums and Archives. Only one of these was less than courteous, and, in the end, gave me no help at all. Sadly, their men's share in the book reflects this, although they performed with distinction before and during the siege.

I must mention the following, with thanks.

Messrs R. H. Fair and Mark Walford for telling me of Captain Edmund Fisher, 1/Manchester Regiment, and Mr. J. T. Stanton for information on Sergeant F. E. Talbot, 42nd Battery, RFA. These gentlemen contacted me and I am very grateful for sight of the fascinating material left by their respective relatives. In Pietermaritzburg is Steve A. Watt, whose photos helped me with the earlier book, and he supplied his photo of Intombi Camp.

The National Army Museum, Chelsea, is always helpful, as is the staff of the Public Library at Stalybridge. Among Regimental Museums, Melanie Brooker, Curator of The Gordon Highlanders Museum, Aberdeen, G. C. Streatfield, Manager/Curator, Soldiers of Gloucestershire Museum, Les Murphy at the Archive of the Devonshire Regiment were all courteous and of great assistance. Dr. Courtney, Newarke House Museum, Leicester kindly gave me access to the Leicestershires' records, and Simon Jones at the Archive of The Kings (Liverpool Regiment) was most hospitable. I am grateful to Col Jacobs and J H du Pisani of the The War Museum of the Boer Republics for further use of their murals as a cover picture, and to Dr. J. Vincent, Province of KwaZulu-Natal Dept of Education and Culture, Museums Department, for photographs. Mr. D. Erasmus, The Natal Witness (South Africa's oldest newspaper - established 1846), was a great help with photos from the newspaper's collection.

Advice for Tourers

The advice in Colenso holds well still, though the remarks about prudence are even more appropriate. Sadly, it seems that there is even greater insecurity in South Africa as a whole but the writer can only say that he has seen nothing dangerous in the countryside on the Battlefield route. Common sense has seen him through.

The subject matter of the earlier Battleground South Africa book was south of Ladysmith, though nearby; so the approach from Durban or Johannesburg had merits. In this case the approach from the north will definitely be the best. Coming from Gauteng tourists have constant foretastes of the campaign. On the roadside direction markers and signposts the names of the various Commandos are reviewed constantly. From Sandspruit travellers are in company with Joubert and the others as Natal is entered.

From the British visitor's point of view the upside of South Africa's current struggle is that billets and rations are even more reasonable in price, and the advice previously given still applies. But again, pay attention to the time and circumstances of intended arrival in the country - or, as a stranger, in any big city there - and, if driving is out of the question, have a room nearby pre-booked. The open road can come after a night's rest.

As before, give the people a chance, white and black alike.

Chapter One

THE BACKGROUND

On the night of 19/20 October 1899, a Boer leader, Lukas Meyer, rode across the veld, accompanied by 4000 horsemen. They dragged with them four field guns and two Maxim guns. They were hidden from public view by the darkness and lashing rain, though it was not as though the populace, such as it was, did not know they were there. The bold invasion had been announced, so tonight's secrecy was tactical, as the objective was the town of Dundee and its British garrison. Daylight would see the first major armed clash of their offensive.

Lukas Meyer.

What had brought them to this, a brazen attack by farmers on the troops and subjects of the most powerful potentate the world had yet seen? To understand we have to go back almost to the beginning of the century.

Road travel in South Africa. This shows the crossing to Zululand by the Lower Tugela Drift in 1879. Things had hardly improved by 1899.
Courtesy of Dr J Vincent, Director, KwaZulu-Natal Museum Service.

The Cape of Good Hope, at the southern tip of the African continent, was well named, as without plenty of hope no man would have ventured past it in the tiny vessels of the seventeenth century. But, trusting in their ships and their captains, great wealth in prospect drove them round into the wild eastern waters. For the British, the attraction was India, and for the Dutch the trade of their own East India Company. Traders were in dire need of a staging post when it is considered that ships from Europe had to go all the way across the Atlantic to the Brazilian coast to catch the trade wind to blow them 'round the corner.' Voyages were measured in months and years, not days and weeks, and the Dutch in particular found a watering-place on what was basically a wild and inhospitable shore, at Table Bay.

In 1652 they sent a surgeon named Jan Van Riebeeck to establish a proper port there, but it was not until the start of the next century that the numbers of settlers began to grow.

Sadly for them, in the last twenty years of the eighteenth century Holland was pushed out of her place in the trading world as Europe became embroiled in the Test Match between France and Britain. When the latter won in 1814, she was awarded the Cape and its hinterland in exchange for £6,000,000.

Unwillingly, there came with it its inhabitants. A rough but capable people, they were deeply religious in the sober Dutch fashion but so self-reliant that Holland's democracy, the only government they wanted, was itself only just tolerable. At that, only if they did not have to pay much.

They had not been happy with the *Verenigde OostIndische Compagnie* (United East India Company), so the British, with their even greater interference and nit picking, were not welcome. One of the prospective points of argument was the treatment of natives. The British in South Africa were in no situation to be holier than the next man, but they and their Bible-Society missionaries were seen by the Boers as meddling, and, no doubt, hypercritical do-gooders. The black workers had a value, but were often treated harshly, at least, by the farmers. Manpower was needed in the wide-open spaces, so the Boers employed 'apprentices'. This was a very suspicious system indeed, and at its worst was a form of slavery, for children taken as prisoners by the Boers were placed in the ranks of the apprentices. In any case, a tradition was building up among the Boers of enforced unpaid labour, as observed by respectable witnesses over the years.

In 1838 the slaves in South Africa were officially free men and women after a four year warning period and many Dutch subjects of the Crown lost a lot of money and found their lives seriously changed. Further, thanks to the influence of 'do-gooders', the government often discriminated against them in their confrontations with difficult natives. (Of course, this unfair discrimination was more than redressed when the Native Lands Act of 1913 came in.) Numbers of Boers set off north, some across the Orange River, and some into Natal, where they had to deal with the powerful Zulu people. There was great hardship but the settlers in the east, after defeating Dingaan at Blood River on 16 December 1838, founded the Republic of Natalia.

The area had seen the great upheaval known as the Mfecane from 1818, the violence caused by Shaka bringing into subjection all his neighbours, and many natives were still moving about in the land. By 1842 the Boers felt that the confusion was so dangerous they began to talk to the British again, leading to the annexation of Natal.

Meanwhile, further west, other trekkers had battled with Mzilikazi's Matabele people (who themselves had dispossessed previous tenants when pushed westward to escape Shaka's attention) and at Bloemfontein Sir Harry Smith, Governor of Natal, proclaimed 'Transorangia' to be the Orange River Sovereignty.

The Boers who had travelled furthest of all, to cross the Vaal River, attempted to end this and Smith had to defeat Andries Pretorius' farmers at Boomplaats in 1848.

The British were in a peculiar position, for those on the spot believed that it was in the Crown's interest to own African land, but the authorities at home were in the 'Little England' phase and wanted no part of African expansion. Things were to change later!

The first meeting of the thirteen-man Legislative Council of the Orange River Sovereignty was held on 1st June 1850 with H. H. D. Warden, the Acting British Resident in Transorangia as President, but, already, Earl Grey was planning to abandon the area.

Queen Victoria's subjects were gradually gaining in prosperity because of the miracle of the industrial revolution, and Britain was introspective.

She was complacent too and, at the top, often incompetent. From our vantage point at the end of the twentieth century, it seems that the British Empire was done-for even in its Victorian heyday. Lordly rulers and their general officers avoided the responsibilities of ownership and oversight while hoping that commercial interests would develop the territories. It looks as though the Empire was thrown away as carelessly as Tommy Atkins was let down. The business was, even then, all about management, and many of the managers were, from generation to generation, bunglers.

This repeatedly showed in South Africa from when the first wave of British immigrants in 1820 were given false hopes and subjected to half-witted plans. Expediency ruled, all the way to the selling out of the non-white inhabitants after the Boer War. Great discredit falls on those who held their titles with incompetence.

In the middle of the nineteenth century Britain was preoccupied with other events distant from home, but much nearer than South Africa. The Crimean War revealed that all was not well with the British Army and its leadership. This would be a shock to the folks at home given that they had known little of the army and had cared even less. Near to or at the bottom of the social heap, were the classes that provided the ordinary soldiery, and the British, warlike though they may have been, had never held either the labouring classes or the ordinary soldiery in high esteem.

For many years the army was ignored, or viewed with suspicion, and when it was billeted nearby it was wished away in 'not in my backyard' fashion. Now they were going to be forced to consider it and what they would learn would be unpleasant, for the army was badly in need of reform.

So, with money to be made out of domestic muck, and worries in the Crimea and at home, the bottom of Africa felt like a responsibility rather than an opportunity. Britain resolved to end her expansion in southern Africa altogether, and at the 1852 Sand River Convention any claim to the Transvaal was given up, with the bonus that, if she abolished slavery, the South African Republic would be allowed to buy gunpowder. The people in the area were split, but the infant republic's Volksraad ratified the deal. Immediately they were involved in war with a chief called Sechele; a name quickly forgotten, but here the names of two Field-Cornets appear that we shall not forget - Paul Kruger and Piet Joubert.

While the Boers in Transvaal were busy at home, things were equally boisterous south of the Vaal.

The British continued their muddled course and on 23 February 1854 at the Bloemfontein Convention, the Queen's servants renounced her sovereignty north of the Orange River. The inhabitants of the country were by no means whole-hearted in their joy at independence but they made the best they could of it and J. P. Hoffman accepted from the people the role of President, and from the King of the Netherlands a design for a flag.

In Britain those thoughtful modernists who could respond to the periodic prods administered by unlooked-for disasters like the Crimean War were made to think. The army, it seemed, was not the capable machine that the Iron Duke had created; it had fallen into decay since Waterloo. The Indian Mutiny then concentrated the mind of the government to consider the question of how big an army the country needed and of what type of men. Even though most of the rulers were gentlemen living off estate rents, and, therefore in management by accident, they began to discern that the principle of entering the management structure by buying your way in was very bad.

Mostly the troops were needed abroad and, behind them, the shortage of good reserves was highlighted. Coming from the least educated classes and signed up for twenty years, when the soldiers returned to civilian life they were of little use as a reserve.

The Orange Free State and the Transvaal were now huge isolated territories where the Boer farmers were again leading their own existence: crude but independent; tough but rewarding. They worked hard and each man had deference to no other: on his own farm he was free to use the whip as law, and did so. Their democratic executives must have had a nightmare making the government work.

The social life was of the simplest, with periodic gatherings at the nearest embryonic town that was growing up round some trading post. Here, in wagon camps, they would mix and pray together, and the young people had a chance to eye one another, the parents a chance to pair them up formally.

An interesting difference with the western United States of the same period was that there was little transfusing by immigration into the society. Apart from the Huguenots long ago, few groups came, although English, Scots, Welsh, Irish and German surnames exist among them. Traders, who were often of these latter races, opened stores near the drifts or crossroads to supply the settlers. It was here where the dorps, or villages, and later, burgs (towns), grew up.

The traders began as aliens, however, so there was no input of new and strange ideas and the thinking remained parochial; the Bible was God's Word and a reading and writing textbook. Book learning stopped when a man could read the Scriptures or check a simple invoice before signing his name.

A bad result of all this self-sufficiency was that a man ignored the law if it suited him, and the taxes did not get paid: a good result was the absence of a class-system such as dominated the British thinking.

By 1859 Pretoria was the capital of the South African Republic where every white man capable of bearing arms had the right to speak in the Volksraad. Paul Kruger was Commandant-General.

Democracy was the life's blood of the Boer people but it also doomed them to constant dissension and little republics came and went while there were numbers on both sides of the Vaal River who would have been glad enough to put up with the British busybodies.

In Europe other nations besides Britain were also faced with 'change and decay' or, if they were more efficient, with change and improvement. The most successful was Prussia, busy improving its army under the guidance of von Moltke and his associates. A feature that served them well was that the units of the army were constructed on a local basis so that appeal was made to that rascally emotion, village patriotism.

In 1868, the Secretary of State for War, Mr. Edward Cardwell, began to reform the British army. In fact, others since the Crimean War had made moves, but after looking into the existing problems, he began to make changes. Men began to be brought home from the colonies, saving money, and then the question of long service was addressed. A bill to change to short service engagements was discussed in Parliament in 1870 with the daily evidence of the Prussians' accomplishment in modernising their army in the papers.

Of course, only a volunteer army was envisioned, as the traditional public attitude meant that conscription on the German model was quite out of the question.

Others went on to complete the work of modernisation.

The old numbered regiments of the line - often single battalion regiments consisting of underpaid, undersized, sometimes starved and often flogged, red-coated 'articles', as the Duke of Wellington once referred to them - disappeared. To some civilians the prospect of regular meals and, sometimes, a dry bed were attractive. Often it was the army that undertook the duty of completing the recruit's physical growth. With all its cruelty, it oversaw his physical development - the only favour it ever did him.

In the place of these, earlier, hapless ones there appeared two-battalion regiments recruited from a geographical area, although the regiment's name could be misleading. Men who likely hailed from the same streets and hills as one another manned them. For example, the York and Lancaster Regiment had little to do with York and certainly nothing to do with Lancaster, but recruited in South Yorkshire - Sheffield, Rotherham, Barnsley etc. It was of two battalions and previously had been the 65th and the 84th Regiments of Foot.

The men were paid and fed better, the discipline was becoming less brutal and they were to be managed not by gentlemen who had bought their commissions, but by professionals, who might still be gentlemen.

As the century wore on and central Africa's wealth uncovered, Europe was more and more deeply involved. Britain felt that, like it or lump it, she must control what was happening so this meant being dragged deeper and deeper in to the affairs of the rickety republics north of the Cape.

In the 1870s 'Federation' became the buzzword. Cape Colony and Natal could be associated with Griqualand West, Kaffraria and Basutoland as clients, and the lands controlled by the powerful native nations like the Zulu, Swazi, Matabele etc., formed into one big group.

Things looked promising by 1877 when the Transvaal was just about bankrupt and the British annexed it with some opposition. The Afrikaner press was acquiescent, and the Executive Council agreed to serve; though Joubert refused and Kruger worked to resurrect independence. British rule put the Transvaal back on an orderly basis before the chance came for the dissenters to wreck what changes had been made. The opportunity appeared for the British to bring down the Zulu King Cetshwayo and his fierce military system, and this presented Joubert and Kruger with their turn.

Britain's start at army reform had come not a moment too soon. Now, in 1879, as she continued to obey the command, 'Rule, Britannia', the old lady was badly bruised by two reverses, one at Isandlwana in Zululand, and another in Afghanistan, at Maiwand. Further indicators flashed indicating that all was still not right, one

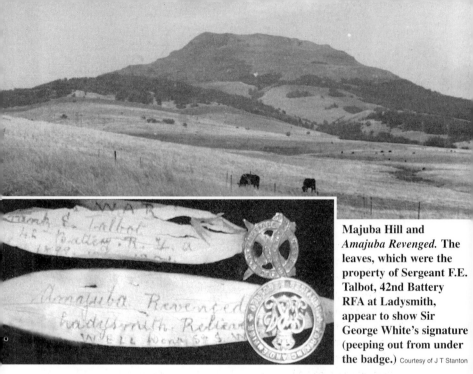

Majuba Hill and *Amajuba Revenged*. The leaves, which were the property of Sergeant F.E. Talbot, 42nd Battery RFA at Ladysmith, appear to show Sir George White's signature (peeping out from under the badge.) Courtesy of J T Stanton

being lit by the Boers at Majuba Hill in 1881 – *Amajuba,* the hill of doves.

While the colonial administrators were distracted in Zululand, Paul Kruger and his associates had gathered strength, and, in December of 1880, two companies of British troops were ambushed and many killed in what could well be described as murder. The British were weak on the ground and badly led, as usual, and their enemy was seriously underestimated, as usual. At home, there was grave division on the matter in the highest places, also as usual. When the Boers had inflicted punishment on the Redcoats at Laing's Nek, at Ingogo, and finally at Majuba Hill on February 27, the new government of Mr. Gladstone retired into Little England and gave the Transvaal back its independence.

The European powers competed throughout the 1880s for portions of the continent, and the British annexed Zululand and added St. Lucia Bay in the east, while taking control of Bechuanaland. By these moves the Germans in the west were prevented from making a border with the South African Republic, and then prevented from getting a foothold between Portuguese East Africa and Natal. Every piece in the White jigsaw at the toe of Africa was now in place, with no place for an independent black man; and so was laid the road-bed to the events of the Twentieth Century.

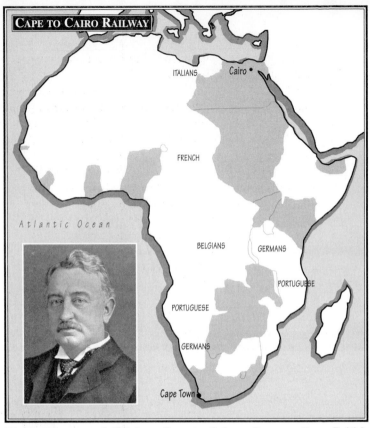

Rhodes' dream unfulfilled; a Cape to Cairo railway – all on British territory. Foiled by Belgians and Germans!

Clearly, Britain had thrown away many of her opportunities and the Boers had set themselves against willing incorporation into the modern world. We shall now see that gold changes everything - and nothing.

Both Boer republics were unhappy with the British again, when, in 1886, the poor and turbulent South African Republic, the Transvaal, found itself the owner of vast gold reserves. Kruger and the conservative majority saw the gold as a mixed blessing giving, on the one hand, solvency, and on the other, opportunity for the introduction of all those influences that would taint their 'pure' life style.

The miners moved in, mainly British, American, Australian and other colonials, known as Uitlanders, as did the investors from Kimberley. The hangers-on, sellers of alcohol and the other fleshly delights, flooded in so that Johannesburg quickly grew into a wild place. The decade closed with the outsiders growing in numbers and usefulness as taxpayers, but more and more restless at having no voice in the country's running.

Kruger could see the obvious danger in giving Uitlanders the vote and he was acutely aware of the imperialist activities of the English adventurer, entrepreneur and politician, Cecil John Rhodes. Later, in 1899, Rhodes was described in the British periodical *Black and White Budget* as the one who,

> 'may be given the full credit of bringing to the front the question of British supremacy in South Africa. He is a son of the parsonage whom weak lungs drove to Africa, where he found health, wealth, and a mission - the latter being the expansion of the British Empire. He has kept his health, he has been generous with his wealth, and he has kept to his purpose. Naturally, he does not like Kruger: naturally, Kruger does not like him. But Rhodes is a strong man and goes his way. If Kruger is in the way - and he is - he goes.'

Kruger, capable and cunning, intransigent yet prepared to use modern technology, imported 13,000 Martini-Henrys in 1894. In 1895 a further 10,000 rifles and twelve million rounds arrived and the artillery makers in Europe, Krupp and Creusot, were contacted.

In this same year, Cecil Rhodes' associates justified Kruger's activity with the infamous Jameson Raid. Laughable if it was not so disgraceful, the invasion of the Transvaal by a gang of Rhodesian

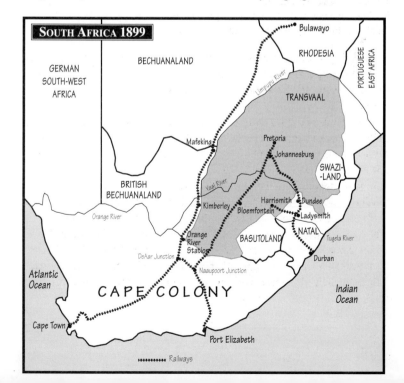

Police ended in surrender at Doornkop on 2 January 1896. Kruger saw to it that not just the British public but Europe's leaders, who he was convinced mattered, knew all about old Albion's perfidy.

Key steps on the road to war were the appointment of Sir Alfred Milner as High Commissioner of South Africa in August 1897 and the winning by Kruger of a fourth term as President in February 1898. This pair seems almost to make a match when it comes to obduracy and guile, but not so, Milner won hands down in his aim of bringing the Boers to the battlefield. If only someone had listened to Lieutenant General Sir W Butler, Britain's Commander in South Africa, who forecast that an army of 200,000 would be called for - and was recalled home.

By 1899, the farmers' republics had up to 80,000 rifles in store, many of them Mausers, the latest of the Victorian age's technology. The 1898 Mauser's magazine took five rounds in a clip all loaded together and their bandoleers became a common feature in the photographs of the contemporary Boers and in modern museums alike. That feed of five rounds at a time, along with the use of "smokeless" cartridges, was to be a tremendous help in the trenches before Colenso and Magersfontein, at Modder River and the Heights of Tugela. Often the British soldiers never even saw the enemy.

In Ladysmith's Siege Museum the claim is even made, 'The Mauser was a more humane weapon than the Martini Henry [British Army issue] because it did not cause large wounds and most wounded men would recover. The bullets could be altered to "dum-dums" which had the same impact as the soft lead bullets of the Martini-Henry.' The Martini-Henry with its 11.4mm bullets, both long barrelled as well as the short barrelled carbine, still used the old black powder, though Alfred Nobel had invented the smokeless explosive ballistite in 1885, calling it after the ballister, or crossbowman.

The Mauser rifle used by the Boers. The cartridges E are carried in a holder, from which, by one pressure of the thumb, they are released and dispose themselves in proper order in the magazine A. They are pressed upwards by a spring B, and forced, one at a time, into the chamber C by the bolt D.

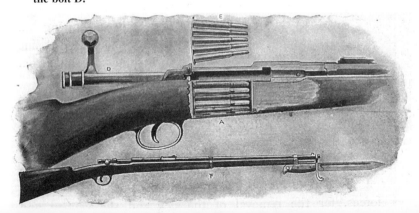

Maxim Gun Detachment at drill.

Pom Pom shell.
Courtesy of 'Natal Witness'.

The evolution of the machine gun reached Helge Palmcrantz's development in 1873 with the finance provided by Thorsten Nordenfeldt and by 1888, Nordenfeldt had teamed up with Hiram Maxim to produce the most advanced machine gun yet. Maxim recognised that the recoil produced by a modern gun could be used to work a belt-fed, semi-automatic, water-cooled gun, and he designed one of 7.69mm calibre firing at 500 rounds per minute.

Then came the recoil-operated automatic gun firing 1lb. explosive shells, and, after Her Majesty's Government rejected this, the Transvaalers quickly booked it in numbers. The fact that they now had plenty of money is evidenced by the cost of operating this 37mm variant - 150 rounds at 6/6d each - £48. 15. 0d. per minute. Once the British had seen its devastating effectiveness they reversed their previous decision and bought 'Pom Poms' by the dozen. So successful was it that by 1898 Hilaire Belloc, in his poem *'The Modern Traveller',* could make the acid observation of mutinous Natives,

> *'Whatever happens we have got*
> *The Maxim gun and they have not.'*

The Boer Presidents' interest in bigger guns brought the latest designs - four huge 155mm Creusot guns

De Fransche Batterij, Transvaal artillery. Courtesy of J T Stanton.

along with four 120mm Krupp howitzers and fourteen 75mm guns from Krupp and Creusot. They complemented five 75mm Vickers-Maxim mountain guns, two of Dr. Jameson's Maxim-Nordenfeldts, twenty-two pom poms and thirty-one Maxim machine guns. All of them used smokeless powder.

The Great Powers in Europe watched closely as the British Colonial Secretary, Joseph Chamberlain, worked at his ambition of welding the entire Cape together as part of the Empire. Chamberlain was clever enough to have avoided implication in the illegal Jameson Raid (though he is now considered to have been in it up to the neck), but was right in the open in his support of the Uitlanders in April 1899.

Black and White Budget was as fulsome in its praise of the Colonial Secretary as it was of Rhodes.

> 'The Right Honourable Joseph Chamberlain, to whom HM has entrusted the care of her colonies, is the Beloved of Birmingham, the Loathed of the Little Englander, and the man whom Kruger fears above all others. He is over sixty, smokes strong tobacco, never takes exercise, grows and wears orchids, and has done more to strengthen the supports of the British flagstaff than any other six of his colleagues in the Cabinet. He can write a stinging dispatch, and he can pick a good servant - e.g. Sir Alfred Milner.'

Milner was also held in high esteem by the 1899 *Black and White*

Budget. At the end of Chamberlain's strong right arm, Milner made sure that all the twists and turns of diplomacy took the Cabinet nearer and nearer to the war that he (Milner) wanted. He believed that this would end with the whole of southern Africa under the Union Jack.

In March 1899 the Uitlanders petitioned the Queen to correct the unfair tax burden and to secure for them the vote. At Bloemfontein in May Milner met with Kruger to bring the latter to accept the viewpoint of Cabinet, while making sure that the old man could not. His actions and those of his master at home ensured that the Transvaalers were intransigent and the British public brought to a state of jingoism. Again, *Black and White Budget* highlighted the received text on the subject of Uncle Paul in that same *Transvaal Special no.1*, saying,

'Stephen John Paul Kruger, President of the South African Republic (better known as the Transvaal) is a heavy looking man who was born on October 10 seventy-four years ago. He crossed the Vaal in the Great Trek of 1839 and from then until now has been a persistent opponent of everything British. 'Oom' Paul became President in 1883, and from that date may be reckoned our chief troubles in South Africa. Long headed, wily, stubborn - 'the battery mule's a mule' - he wields a tremendous power over the Boers and what he wants they do. To the British in the Republic, he is a bogey and nurses use his name to frighten Outlander babies. He once called our Queen 'een kwaje vrouw' (which neither sounds nor means nice), and we haven't forgotten it. He hates Chamberlain, Rhodes, and Milner, just as he hates everything British and he often preaches o' Sundays [sic], his sermons generally being a glorification of the Boer and a sweeping damnation of the Briton. For an old man, he ought to know better.'

One of the Boers' armoury of Krupp manufactured guns.

Gradually, Kruger gave ground but only as far as Milner wished, so that the picture of stubbornness could be sustained with the British Public. Chamberlain, thinking that he was in control, and that Paul would in the end back-off and give the Uitlanders the vote, felt ready in September to force Lord Salisbury's Cabinet to act. It was decided that 10,000 men be sent to Natal.

Here Kruger dug in his feet. It may have surprised Chamberlain, but not Milner, for he knew the Boers would fight. He had worked tirelessly for that aim, dragging his feet when applying the Colonial Office's instructions on the one hand, making it hard for Kruger to be conciliatory on the other. The conference that was to have settled things broke down in June 1899 and the British garrison of 10,000 or so men was faced with 50,000 well armed mounted infantry. At the end of September, President Kruger prepared an ultimatum to give to the mighty British Empire requiring her to remove the troops near to the border with the South African Republic. It was eventually delivered on October 9 and would run out on October 11. General Sir W. Penn Symons, commanding in Natal, wanted a further 5600 men to secure the northeastern corner of that province and they started to trickle in by the end of the month.

But it would be a month before sufficient troops were on the ground and while 'The Public' in Britain was prepared, the Government was not. Those who directed the nation's affairs had gone through the whole tortuous process of diplomacy while knowing that the troops were in the wrong place with the wrong equipment and the wrong training. There were shortages in stores of essential supplies, and the key tools, modern guns and ammunition, were in short supply or even not available. The official reports have long since come into the public domain and the penny-pinching has a surprisingly modern feel about it. Interestingly, the 'Ladysmith Lyre', a humorous and sardonic paper published in the town during the siege said, as a 'news' item in an early addition, 'The artillery intended for the campaign in South Africa will be dispatched as soon as the necessary ammunition has been received from the German factories.'

Those with executive power were divided. The War Minister was The Marquis of Lansdowne, KG, GCSI, GCMG, owner of vast lands in Britain and Ireland, and unimpressive. His Commander in Chief and critic, the most famous general of his day, was Lord Wolseley, a fighting soldier. He believed that a war in South Africa was just what the army, reformed and wanting more reform, needed. And yet Wolseley was unhappy. He knew that the Boers could not be beaten without the sternest efforts and if the job were to be done thoroughly from day one, cash and imagination would be required. Lansdowne did not want to part with the former and had none of the latter to give away.

The British man in the street, who did not have to fight, was ebullient about things, for Majuba Hill had not been forgotten or forgiven. Gladstone's settlement with the Boers in 1881 was, to many, odious. Righteous indignation and bile now poured forth and the rightness or wrongness of Boer conduct was laced with a liberal dose of nationalism. Not Liberal with a large 'L' of course, for many of the anti-war group that emerged were in that party, which had made the Peace of 1881.

Marquis of Lansdowne KG GCSI GCMG.

The newspapers played their usual role of whipping up popular opinion for the cause and the *Illustrated Mail* **WAR NUMBER** of November 1899 was headlined in bold capitals, 'We Must Help The Girl That Tommy Left Behind Him'. There was a full-page drawing of a woman carrying a babe and dragging a small girl, while at her side a boy in a sailor suit tootled his tin trumpet. Featured below is Rudyard Kipling's *'The Absent-Minded Beggar.'* It opens -

> 'When you've shouted 'Rule Britannia'-
> when you've sung 'God save the Queen' -
> When you've finished killing Kruger with your mouth -
> Will you kindly drop a shilling in my little tambourine
> For a gentleman in kharki [sic] ordered South?'

- and goes on to eulogise him.

'Tommy Atkins' was now the popular name for the British soldier, the 'gentleman in kharki,' and the sentiments expressed tell some truth about him, but the objective was to bring the waverers in to the fold and their pennies into the collecting tins.

Journalists carried on the good work and the first reports of actions would often speak of sensational victories, only for the hyperbole to be modified later, and be contradicted by history later still. We shall come across examples.

The attitude of the literate lower classes is expressed in offerings to be found in the pages of the newspapers and the following, in a northern weekly paper of the time, is typical.

BRITONS v. BOERS.
Shall nation strive with nation
For justice, peace and right?
Shall nation vie with nation,
And put their foes to flight?
Fear not the day of battle,
Ye Britons bold and brave,
For British rule must triumph,
Where Britain's flag doth wave.

The second verse refers to the 'mighty Kruger', and the last exhorts Sons of Britain not to shrink duty's call so that,

'as the great Majuba Hill,
so the victory will be ours;
Let harmony once more prevail
'Twixt Britain and the Boers.'

Commercial Houses also quickly took up the theme for the sake of their products, including tobacco and prophylactic and restorative supplies like this ointment:

HOMOCEA FOR THE BATTLEFIELD
NOTICE
___

TROOPS FOR THE TRANSVAAL SHOULD WITHOUT FAIL BE PROVIDED WITH HOMOCEA, AS THERE IS NOTHING MORE SOOTHING OR HEALING KNOWN.

FOR WOUNDS, CUTS, BRUISES, BROKEN SKIN, SORE PLACES GENERALLY, USE HOMOCEA OFTEN, AND PLENTY OF IT.

INFANTRY NEED HOMOCEA FOR ANOINTING THE FEET ON THE MARCH, AND FOR SORES CAUSED BY CHAFING ACCOUTREMENTS.

CAVALRY NEED HOMOCEA FOR TROUBLES CAUSED BY ROUGH RIDING, DAMP SADDLES, ETC., AND ESPECIALLY FOR PILES.

SEE THAT NO FRIEND GOES TO THE FRONT WITHOUT HOMOCEA. WHAT ELSE CAN THEY RELY ON TO TOUCH THE SPOT 'AND SOOTHE THE ACHING PART?'

But as a few at the top, like Butler, Wolseley and Sir Redvers Buller, listened to these sudden eulogies (would the reading of advertisements be beneath them?), they were aware of the fact that with all the modifications to its structure, the British Army might have further lessons to learn. Since Wellington's time the methods used in set-piece battles by all the European powers had hardly changed; firstly the artillery, which grew in calibre and skill as the century wore on, 'softened up' the enemy in an exchange of fire. Then, infantry would be thrown in, in numbers and in close order, volley firing, before finishing the job with the bayonet.

The cavalry, waiting on the flank until called on stage, then fell on an enemy bludgeoned by the guns and overwhelmed by the hand to hand fighting. As they finally broke and turned away, the horsemen with lance or sabre were loosed among those fleeing.

This was how the job was done and the rules were familiar to all Europeans, gentleman-officers and private soldiers alike. These rules were not acceptable, however, to the Boers.

They were not horse-soldiers because they fought on foot; nor were they foot soldiers either, for they arrived on ponies. They were afraid, it was said, of the bayonet, but were peerless marksmen. While they acknowledged the endless patience, bravery and honest obedience of the British soldier and his Colonial allies, they matched it with field-craft and the ability to appear and disappear at will and, once 'in the ring', to shoot straight.

Every thing about the Boer army was different from a European army. Every male between sixteen and sixty, old enough to carry a gun,

Boys of sixteen as well as many grey-bearded men were found in the ranks of the Boers.

was to be armed and equipped, ready to report at a moment's notice. Those from 18 to 34 could be called out first, then 34 to 50, and, in the end, the ones below 18 and over fifty. Refusal meant a fine of £37.10.0, or three months in prison.

The burghers assembled without uniform and recognised that the community had a right to requisition all private property in wartime, but they organised themselves on democratic lines, following leaders that they themselves had voted in.

The burghers of the Transvaal elected a Commandant-General for a ten-year term with, in wartime, co-opted assistant generals, supported by a civilian secretary and ten clerks. The Orange Free State was even less of a war machine, for it only had a Commandant-in-Chief in time of war, elected by the commandants and field-cornets.

Each of the 22 electoral districts of the Transvaal and the 18 of the Orange Free State produced a commando, which could be as small as 300 strong or as great as 3000.

The Commandant was a purely military officer elected by the burghers in the district, serving a five-year term in the Transvaal and three years in Orange Free State. A district was divided into two to five wards, each of which appointed a Field-Cornet for a three year term, serving as a Government Officer and Justice of the Peace. He kept the register of the burghers and made sure that all were mounted and

Boer 'Sharpshooters' wait for the Khakis.

equipped, reporting the condition of his ward to the government at three monthly intervals. In the field he was aided by elected assistant field-cornets and several corporals who distributed the rations, animal feed, clothing and ammunition supplied by the commissariat officer.

The Field-Cornet was the key figure upon whom any organisation in the usual military sense fell. Besides keeping the register and reporting to the government he was responsible for securing, either from the government, or by commandeering, ammunition and supplies - as well as the transport to carry them to the men. With all these responsibilities he even produced the men, for his was the task of calling them out from their homes to report, mounted, with arms and a day's rations.

All the men were riders and hunters so horse and man made a team, and the only training was to 'keep their eye in' as marksmen. To complete the picture, they could live so simply that mealie-meal (ground cooked maize), biltong (meat sun-dried in thin strips) and coffee would keep them going for days.

This was all very different from the cart-loads of delicacies and appurtenances that British officers required, and so much more efficient than the stop-start starvation that their men endured

This citizen/bucolic army was stiffened up by the Transvaal and Swaziland police, who numbered about 1800 men, and by foreign contingents. Germans, Irish-Americans, Scandinavians, Dutch and Frenchmen were there, either because they had a personal hatred of Britain, or maybe just because she was the most successful nation on earth. Possibly the best known of these mercenaries was Colonel de Villebois-Mareuil, the chamber pot man.

A most valuable service provided by the foreigners was that of organizing and officering the artillery, typically the famous Major Albrecht who had led the Free State Artillery since 1880. The gunners, however, had something to learn from the Boers and they adapted to

Father and sons on commando.

On outpost duty before Ladysmith.

the mobile style of fighting that the 'infantry' employed.

Of the generals, Piet Joubert was too old. Always cautious, and owner of the Boer nickname of 'Slim' or 'Wily' Piet, he now appeared to have no dynamism left, with many of his men wasting their time in the laagers round Ladysmith when Botha could have used them elsewhere. Cronje, too, failed in the end. He was master of his men, but allowed himself to be trapped and captured at Paardeberg, and that was only the start. He went into dignified imprisonment but, after the war, followed Sitting Bull into the American Circus arena where, with a body of ex-combatants of both sides, he relived Colenso and Paardeberg for the sake of the thrill seeking American public.

The most successful leaders were Louis Botha, Christian de Wet and De La Rey and they all suffered from being shackled by their own democratic system.

Riflemen, first and last, were the Boers. General Buller warned his soldiers that they would not get close in, and this warning was given because of his own experience when fighting alongside men like Piet Uys in the Zulu War of 1879. The Boers were not interested in using the bayonets supplied with the Mausers as offensive weapons, but rather preferred to use the ground and the atmosphere. They fired their smokeless bullets from trenches and well-built sangars, dug by black forced labour, and the enemy had no idea of their strength.

When the game was up they did not wait to take the bayonet, but, instead, they melted away.

So, knowing that the trickle of disciplined British soldiers would clearly turn into a flood, these armies of horse-soldiers, Transvaalers and troops of the less willing President Steyn of the Orange Free State alike, were instructed to move.

All that was why Lukas Meyer came to be out in the night, in the rain.

Chapter Two

Talana Hill 20 October 1899

We have spent quite some time discovering why Lukas Meyer did not go to bed on the night of 19 October 1899, but it must have felt a longer time to the General himself. It was a black night with torrents of rain. The army had been on the move since the expiry of the ultimatum and the Boers had been poised since the start of the month to the north and west of that Natal 'thumb' that pushes northwards between the Orange Free State and the Transvaal. Meyer moved to the Doornberg area with the Pietretief, Vryheid and Utrecht commandos while Joubert, with some 8000-9000 men, two batteries of field artillery and three 155mm Creusots, was at Sandspruit, north of Volksrust on what is now the R23. Generals Kok and Viljoen were at the bottom of Botha's Pass, west of Newcastle, and the Free State's Chief Commandant, Marthinius Prinsloo, was at Van Reenan's Pass with over six thousand men from Bethlehem, Harrismith, Heilbron, Kroonstad, Vrede and Winburg.

On 7 October, the British General Sir George White had arrived from the War Office. A soldier since 1853, he had won the Victoria Cross after an incident in the Afghan War of 1879/80, since when he had climbed steadily to be Commander in Chief in India. He was a Gordon Highlander who had once led a charge with the cry, 'We must chalk 92nd on those guns!' Like so many of the figures in the war, he was an Irishman, and out of his portrait there stares a gentlemanly figure who was now to command all British forces in Natal.

He was, therefore, senior to General Sir W. Penn Symons and the new commander did not agree with the existing plan to defend the Colony as far north as Newcastle. Two days after arriving

General Sir George Stewart White, VC GCB GCSI GCMG

in South Africa, White and Sir Archibald Hunter met with the Governor of Natal, Sir Walter Hely-Hutchinson. White and Hunter wished to withdraw from the Glencoe area, which meant giving up to the Boers the Biggarsberg Mountains which make a hook east and south-east to the north of Ladysmith.

The Governor's argument overpowered White's, and he agreed that because of the political situation, there could be no withdrawal. Penn Symons was to remain the northern outpost of the British forces, as he wished.

Sir Walter Hely-Hutchinson GCMG, Governor of Natal.

Major-General Sir W Penn Symons.

This general, described as 'dashing', had with him in the Glencoe area the 18th Hussars, a squadron of Natal Carbineers and a contingent of Natal Police. His eighteen guns were those of the 13th, 67th and 69th batteries Royal Field Artillery, and his infantry were the 1/Leicesters, 1/King's Royal Rifles and 2/Dublin Fusiliers. On the 16th the 1/Irish Fusiliers augmented them.

The two guns of the 67th battery RHA which fired the first rounds at Talana Hill. Courtesy of Natal Witness

67th Battery, RFA. Courtesy of Dr J Vincent, Director, KwaZulu-Natal Museum Service.

By the 15th Commandant Erasmus, with 4000 Pretoria, Heidelberg and Boksburg men, was in Newcastle collecting stores left by the British. 'Maroola' Erasmus was an experienced soldier in the Boer fashion who had earned the nickname from some adventure involving a tree of the same name.

If the area is approached from Johannesburg via the R23, the traveller will pass Sandspruit, where Joubert camped before moving with his wife, a powerful woman, and the army to the little town of Volksrust. Leaving town, a right onto the N11, southbound, very quickly brings the visitor to Majuba Hill and there is a rough track up, though when the author passed that way it was not suitable for a conventional car. O'Niel's Cottage, where the Peace Treaty was signed in 1881, is to the right of the road, and the visitor is then coming down Laing's Nek following Joubert's halting advance towards Newcastle.

It is a beautiful drive that compensates for the rather featureless veld traversed after the urban sprawl of Gauteng as far as the Drakensberg. Though not the same as the run down from the Scottish border to Newcastle upon Tyne, there are similar long views and unfolding vales, and the country rolls between great green knobs. (Why should the valley of the Ingogo River or that of the Klip River sound more exotic than those of the Coquet, Kielder or Blyth?) The driver must take care, though, as the historical interest and the view could divert the attention from what is a busy and steep pass.

Newcastle itself, though in a mining area, is not like its Northumberland inspiration. No Tyne Bridge and no Magpies, but there is sunshine for much of the time and the pits from here down to Elandslaagte are surrounded by amiable farmland. There are interesting relics of the period before and after the invasion, like Fort

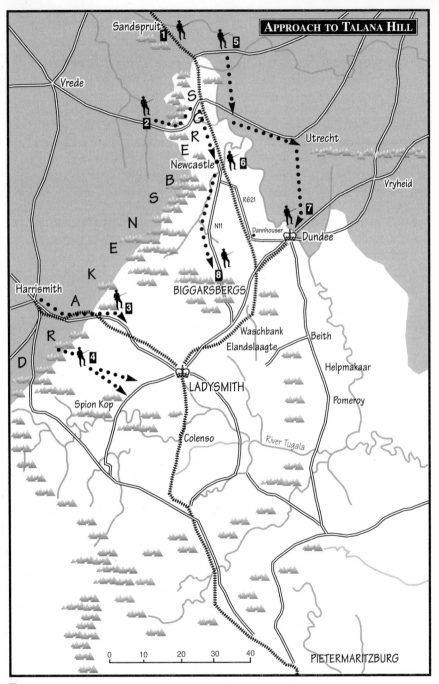

APPROACH TO TALANA HILL

1 **1 October.** Joubert at Sandspruit

2 **12 October.** Kok invades down Botha's Pass.

3 **12 October.** Prinsloo invades down Van Reenan's.

4 **12 October.** Boer Column invades down Tintwa Pass.

5 **1 to 12 October.** Meyer

6 **15 October.** Kok at Newcastle 16 Joubert at Newcastle

7 **20 October.** Meyer arrives at Talana via De Jager's Drift.

8 **18 October** Kok crosses Biggarsbergs via Mkupe Pass.

++++++Railways

British Garrisons: Dundee & Ladysmi

Boers

Amiel, and south of town is the old home of Sir Henry Rider Haggard, though it is a private residence. Famous for 'King Solomon's Mines', 'Alan Quartermain', 'Nada the Lily' and the rest, he was also the young man who ran up the Union Flag for Sir Theophilus Shepstone at the annexation of the Transvaal in April 1877. [Who reads his work now? In spite of his 'noble savages', like Umslopogaas, or perhaps because of them, fifty years ago he first generated the author's interest in South Africa and in the condition of its native people.]

Leaving Newcastle, the 'invader's road' is the N11 for approximately fifteen kilometres, before joining the R621 which bears left via Dannhouser to Dundee a further forty-three km away.

On 15 October, Kok arrived at Newcastle, followed by Joubert the next day. By the 18th Erasmus was at Hattingspruit (fifteen kilometres north of Dundee on today's R621), Prinsloo was down from Van Reenan's and approaching Ladysmith from the west, while Kok was pressing on roughly down the line of today's N11 over Mkupe Pass. As Erasmus set off on the last lap for Dundee, Kok was cutting the railway line at Elandslaagte, thus capturing the coalmines there.

At Dundee was the farm of a Scotsman, Peter Smith, who had come to Africa from Tayside and built himself a home in the third quarter of the nineteenth century. He built a family in it also, and eventually a graveyard there as the area developed into an industrial town and farming centre.

In spite of its own railway and the industry the place is entirely unlike Smith's home, for this Dundee has a country air, but not Scottish; rather English Home Counties at one end of town. Here the main shopping street eases its way into the atmosphere of Surrey with the Royal Lion Pub and Restaurant (decor on a Rorke's Drift theme) on the left, and an ornamental garden opposite; a manicured version of a village green in front of the Information Office. The Royal Lion does a good dinner, and a gourmet meal can be eaten in a restaurant near the Information Office, which is near to the Police Station. Also nearby is the Anglican Church of St. James, gently pretty in muted green and white; though somehow un-English in these colours. We shall be back there with tragedy in a little while.

Why should the pub not have a Rorke's Drift theme, when that outpost and lonely Isandlwana are both but seventy or so kilometres away?[1] Yet Dundee has less of a frontier feel and more that of settled suburbia's edge, the pit office a carriage-ride away and the first fields beckoning.

There are numbers of places to stay in the area; at this end of town, apart from the Royal Lion, there are pleasant B & Bs - typically about £20 per night lump sum for two persons, with a beautiful room en suite and a sumptuous breakfast. There will probably be a garden all around the house with an aviary at one end and a swimming pool.

At the other end of the main street it is quite different, for after the stop-lights, or 'robots' as the South Africans call them, Africa reveals her other faces again; not struggling-but-successful Colonial, but plain struggling native or transplanted Asian where life means business, and business may mean life. There are great oriental food-stores - as if in the English Black Country - and street traders, all selling mountains of oranges, or what is in season, on the pavement edge; surrounded by blowing polythene bags, fruit waste and children. Women thread their way in all directions with sacks and other items on their heads, backs die-straight, and often the bags are 10kg and more. Once the writer and his wife saw a straight lissom beauty come out of a shop with a polythene-wrapped sewing machine on her head, brand new and fearfully at risk.

Dundee is comprehensively overlooked. To the north is the bulk of Impati Mountain, 400 metres above the town and five kms away, with the Newcastle road a shoulder strap on its left-hand slope. About one kilometre to the east is Talana Hill, 60 metres above town, on the side of which Mr. Smith sited his farm, and its southern neighbour, Lennox, a similar height above and distant from town. Between them, the road east climbs over the saddle (Smith's Nek) leading to the open veld, while the road south to Helpmekaar separates Lennox from the even bigger pile of the ridge of Indumeni, which is south of town. This eminence has northern skirts about 4 kilometres from town and 200 metres above it.

To the west, the Glencoe road climbs over the curtain of high

Talana Hill today, Smiths Farm buildings on the right.

SMITHS FARM

ground that fills the gap between Impati and Indumeni, and completes the whole 'ring'. Hence, when Colonel de Villebois-Mareuil was in town after the British conceded it, he would graphically suggest that the defenders were in the bottom of a chamber pot.

The way leads down the hill past this area in the morning, just as surely as it would be avoided at night, and the drive is towards Vryheid, but only for ten minutes, as far as Mr. Smith's little settlement, still discrete from the hubbub of the town. Back to the left is the dominating bulk of Impati, and, as the road flattens off through a stand of trees. To the right front is Lennox, a green hump; in front, Smith's farm in the shelter of the hog's back of Talana. The old Scot would surely be displeased now because as the bridge over the Sandspruit is crossed a considerable shantytown is seen on the western shoulder of the hill. [Smith would, however, have recognised the dexterity of young African womanhood as, by the time we got there after an interminable visit to the bank, we found our budding seamstress tripping carelessly over the roughs toward the shanties. The sewing machine was still secure on her proud head supported by that lovely shock-absorbing neck.]

Turn off the road and up the rough drive to the Henderson Hall, with a reconstruction of a 1906 winding house. It is a modern but tasteful looking building housing a coal mining museum, a glass collection and the reconstruction of a section of Dundee in 1912. It has a very interesting display.

To its right there is a pre-1914 cottage, which is arranged as a mine secretary's home and office circa 1920, with a tearoom preparing simple meals and grills in one of the rooms. This would be a suitable place for a light lunch as the whole site will fill in at least a long morning, maybe most of a day.

The wood of tall gum trees is directly at the back of these buildings and the cemetery to their upper left. Here are the Smiths, the McPhails (McPhail was old Smith's son-in-law), and others, besides a number of British soldiers whose lives ended on Talana on 20 October 1899. To the left again is the milking shed, now housing a shop and a display of farm carts; and again an older barn, dating right back to the start, then Smith's Farmhouse, and as the far left outlier, the workshop of 1864. Below them is the coach-house, and lastly, but importantly to students, Talana House with its servants' quarters (now the Public Toilets), and a Coolroom.

Smith's son built Talana House before the Boer War, when a Smith was somebody in these parts. Many famous visitors have been since the war, and now it is the focus of a splendid museum dedicated to local history. As this area has seen much that was seminal to the growth of the Republic, there is plenty to study. Entering, the cave dwellings of the prehistoric inhabitants of the Biggarsberg are seen before passing through into a quite detailed section on the growth of Zulu power. A display highlights the fearful abilities of Shaka and the development of the regimental system, the 'Impis', and their battle-formation that was the basis of his strength. His assassination and the succession leading to his people's collision with the Voortrekkers brings the visitor to the Anglo-Zulu War and a number of interesting displays, uniforms, maps, plans and photographs. Noting the blood-curdling dishonesty of the British Government to bring down Cetshweyo and castrate his house, the student is prepared for the British methods to bring the Boers to war. There are displays on Talana, Elandslaagte, the effects of Boer occupation and the recovery

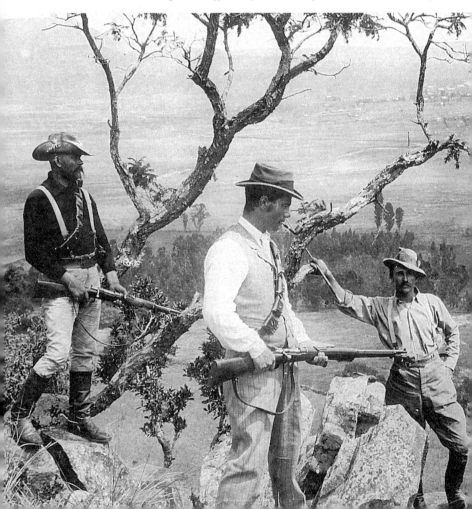

From Talana Hill Meyer would have had a fine view of all the town.

of the town by British troops. This museum should not be missed; it is an essential prelude to a climb up the hill as there is much on-the-spot explanatory comment, many illustrations and models.

General Lukas Meyer and his men are said to have left their camps at 6 pm and crossed De Jager's Drift at nine o'clock on the darkest of rainy nights. There was an encounter with a party of mounted Royal Dublin Fusiliers, which alerted General Penn Symons, so it should have been no surprise that the enemy were ascending Talana Hill. They arrived at the flat summit before dawn on October 20.

From there, when it became light, Meyer would have a fine view of all the town and the British camp, and General Sir George White's greatest fears for the forward position of his forces would be realized.

Meyer sent up the eastern face the 900 man Utrecht Commando under Commandant Hattingh, Commandant Joshua

Boers on Talana Hill.

39

Joubert with the 600 from Wakkerstroom. With them struggled Major Wolmarans with three field guns and a Maxim. Meyer himself with the Middleburg, Pietretief and Vryheid men occupied Lennox Hill and those immediately beyond.

In front of the burghers was a very steep bank falling 50 metres to a terrace some 50 - 70 metres wide which is exposed to the brow of the hill, but with a low stone wall on its outside edge covering a further steep incline beyond. Any British assault on the Boer position could use the wall as protection, though the attackers would still be targets from positions on Lennox Hill as well as from one section of the ridge itself. At right angles, several farm walls ran down the hill, affording some cover to a storming-party, and lower than this were Smith's Farm and the eucalyptus wood 120 metres below the summit, before open land sloped down again to the river.

Now, one hundred years on, the scenery has changed, as with many of the Boer War Battlefields. What often looks in the old photos to be bare and barren land, without concealment, is clothed in scrub, bushes and low, stunted trees and is generally possessed of plenty of cover. But even in October 1899, when there was less scrub, there would be the long, dry, dead grass from last season, cloaking the treacherous rocks from view. How the infantryman could dodge the missiles, make headway and still keep his footing among them is a mystery.

The thick cloud and mist still, at this point, separated the camp from the invaders. Under the low canopy, the men paraded at their camp west of town and, within fifteen minutes Wolmarans' field guns opened the Boer innings. Two 'firsts' were now experienced by those present. Outside India, British troops had always fought in red coats, but now were in khaki, and, also, this would be the first time that a European army had faced the new German magazine-fed rifles. Both facts are significant.

The tiny figures of the attackers could be seen on the hill and there was temporary confusion in the camp, but one British battery was brought into action immediately, and the other galloped hurriedly forward. Some accounts say that they began firing at about six am, and some at 6.20, but whichever is correct, they speedily put Major Wolmarans out of the reckoning, forcing him back.

Symons was at Dundee because he believed that the British should be occupying a forward position, and today his conduct fitted in with his dashing, or reckless, reputation. Within another half-hour, Lieutenant Colonel B. D. Möller had taken the 18th Hussars and

Mounted Infantry round the northern end of Talana to be ready to harass the Boers' retreat. Riding up the valley of the Sand River, they turned right, climbing, and took position right behind Talana Hill. Möller had three options: drive off the Boer horses that were tethered in front of him; wait to ambush the riflemen as they attempted to remount and make off; or dismount and assault the rear of the hill.

Symons decided to attempt an assault of the hill, and everything appeared to be as in the textbook: silence the enemy guns, charge the defenders with the bayonet and drive them back onto the swords of the cavalry.

The infantry marched out of camp and along the de Jager's Drift Road, past the place of today's in-season fruit and all-season polythene, described earlier, and down the hill through the trees to a clearer view of Smith's or Smit's place. The Leicesters and the 67th Battery were left in camp, bearing in mind that Commandant Erasmus was on Impati Hill to the north. The townsmen and women, disturbed by the cannon, and now faced with the well-advertised Boer invasion, cheered the troops on. The meandering spruit runs in the bottom of its cutting, and this, as so often in the war, and to both sides, gave shelter to the men as they lined up to face the foe.

The King's Royal Rifles were on the right and the Dublin Fusiliers on the left, followed by the Irish Fusiliers. Looking at the map, we may ask why there was no attempt to climb the northern end of the hill and 'unroll' the Boer line from that end. A flank attack there would be out of the way of Lukas Meyer and the rest of the force in the Lennox Hill area, and the Boers would have had been targeted from two fronts, as the British were to be in a frontal attack. However, that ploy was not used and the men were sent over the top of the riverbank and straight up the grassy slope towards Smit's Farm, as the enemy called it. Penn Symons seems almost as profligate with other people's lives as Kitchener was at Paardeberg, or Rawlinson and Haig at the Somme.

In the event, weathering the storm of Mauser fire, and the pom poms that were turned on them from above and from Lennox, they reached the wood surrounding the farm and outbuildings by about 7.30 am. Some sort of response to those on Lennox was forthcoming, as the two available batteries had been brought up to a position behind the

41

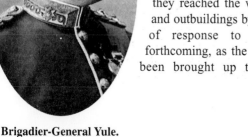

Brigadier-General Yule.

Sandspruit. While the 69th played on Talana, the 13th dealt with Lennox.

In fact, steady Boer rifle fire was now also coming from behind the wall at the foot of the hill's crown. By 8.00 am there were lined along the lower wall and hedge from left to right, 1/Royal Irish Fusiliers, 2/Dublin Fusiliers, 1/King's Royal Rifles. Each battalion's Maxim Gun was at the right hand (SE) end of the wood to tackle Smith's Nek and Lennox Hill (see map). The wood afforded a semblance of cover and the men would not move forward in spite of Brigadier-General James Yule's orders.

The wood, buildings and cemetery are still there, as noted earlier, and wind through the mature trees provides just about the only noise. Although the visitor is in a graveyard, it is pleasant. Looking back down to the road, it is still like open parkland and any attackers would be very exposed now. Turning round and looking up at the hill whose shelter attracted Mr. Smith, we can only see it between the trees, lower growth, farm buildings and, since October 1899, monuments. With the trees above their heads riddled by rifle bullets, and having rushed across the lower slope, it is easy to understand the troops' reluctance.

A sign directs the walker to climb the hill itself at the rear of the cemetery, in fact on the line of the King's Royal Rifle Corps' assault. It looks like the easiest route - not that there is an easy route, but looking to the left the 1st Royal Irish and 1st Dublin Fusiliers had a longer and much harder climb. This one is hard enough.

First, on leaving the doubtful protection of the trees, you are in clear view of the crest-line, so under fire. The writer was deeply conscious of this while struggling forward with two cameras, binoculars, haversack and walking stick. Invisible Boers peopled the ridge and the remnants of the wall below it. This is very like moorland areas familiar to thousands of city children in the north of England. On Saturdays, generations of them have been taken to ramble and scramble and generally let off steam in similar surroundings. There are the same semi-ruined walls for patchy shelter, the same bald patches where one is visible right into the next county, and the same clumps of scrubby trees to pause while the bursting heart settles down. On t'moors, though, they do not have the heat, nor are these primeval lumps of rock hidden by that infernal long grass. Let sheep be praised!

Mercifully, one reaches what seems to be dead ground: a welcome respite for then one faces the terrace across the width of the hill and in full view of the crest. It is impossible to move forward without exposure: hence Penn Symons' problem.

At 9.00 am he rode up to discover the reason for the delay and found himself to be among the Royal Irish Fusiliers. Disdaining advice, he went on through the wood out onto the moor, and there, unseen by his men, he was shot. He bore himself up as he returned, but once out of sight he was taken, dying, to the Field Hospital.

The trouble began for him much lower down the hill than might be expected from reading the reports. This could be because the accounts of the assault start from a lower position. We have, after all, crossed the river by a road bridge with white houses on an estate to our right, Talana to our left with the distant shantytown. Tommy Atkins struggled through the drift and was climbing straight away, under fire in the cornfield where the patient stretcher-bearers ('body snatchers', said the men) found their first customers to conduct back and out of the war. So, Penn Symons' fate was maybe higher up in his terms than it is in ours. He was away to the left of us on the line of the KRRC's advance; his cairn marks a spot at the back of Talana House and

Penn Symons is mortally wounded.

Penn Symons' Cairn. 'On this spot Lieut. Gen. Sir W. Penn Symons fell mortally wounded 20 October 1899. Erected by the Durham Light Infantry'.

we are already far in front of it on this 'killing-ground' of a terrace. It should not be forgotten, either, that at this time Lennox had the field in view from the side to add to the soldiers' problems.

The wall on the main terrace below the crest was taken at 9.30 to 10.00. The Irishmen were to the left, in a donga or depression, with two companies of Irish Fusiliers and the King's Royal Rifles on their right. The men were much troubled by the noise of the pom pom and asked why they had no gun like that: a fair question, since the British had rejected it. The shelter offered by the donga ran out and Captain Weldon was killed as he tried to save his servant, 5078 Private Gorman. Weldon was the first mortality suffered by the Dublins and left a fox terrier called Rose, which sat by him until saved and claimed by the men. Of the KRRC, Captain Pechell and Lieutenant Taylor were killed at the upper wall and Major Boultbee was wounded. Later, Colonel Sherston died in the final assault. At that time many Boers stood up to fire and were seen by the soldiers to be wearing ordinary raincoats and slouch hats. Colonel 'Bobby' Gunning KRRC, who led the last rush, was killed at the crest as well and Lieutenant Norman Hambro was killed by British shrapnel. The Boers meanwhile lost 40 or 50 men including Field-Cornet Sassenbey of Wakkerstroom.

However, once across the flattish terrace the problem is how to get up the last punishing scarp. Even over the flat, the accursed boulders are there, and when climbing it is impossible to concentrate on anything but the climb. The writer went up in ten minutes, laden as earlier described. Every second of it was hateful, but probably a fit youngster, even with a rifle and accoutrements, would do it in three

View from Talana Hill.

LENNOX HILL

TO DUNDEE

TO SMITH'S NEK

EXPOSED TERRACE

Storming Talana Hill.

minutes. He would have to concentrate though and the rain of bullets would make that difficult, as would, in this section, the British shrapnel, tardy in moving forward up the hill.

As the summit was taken, the Boers having left, British artillery was still shelling, and their own guns threatened the British. Private Flynne jumped up, waving to the gunners to warn them, and, as he could not get their attention, he calmly went down the hill ignoring enemy and 'friendly' fire alike, to tell them to lengthen their range. As if this was not enough, the men had not eaten for ten hours and as the action petered out they were marched home in the rain.

The top is a plateau, sloping up at the north end, and the back face is gentler than that facing Dundee, looking away towards the open veld and the wet nights. Towards Transvaal. Everything is exposed to Lennox. This will have been checked with the fine exhibit in the museum and, if the visitor is there in late September he or she is in no

SMITHS FARM

The cross marks where Lieutenant Colonel RH Gunning fell.

Courtesy of Dr J Vincent - Director, KwaZulu-Natal Museum Service

*doubt as to which is Impati, for it is wreathed in the smoke of grass
fires as the old dead growth is burned off to give a start to the tender
new grass awaiting the October rain.*

*The stone walls are still there though the donga at the left-hand end,
where Weldon was killed, is now overgrown, as is the ruined wall at the
top of which Lieutenant Colonel Gunning lost his life. Their memorials
are in the small graveyard at the bottom of the hill with Pechell and
Taylor, near to Colonel Sherston, Yule's Brigade Major and nephew of
Lord Roberts.*

*Interestingly, on the summit there are defences built by the British
in 1900. It may be said that they could have saved Penn Symons, had
he thought of them; but then it would have to be asked, 'what if the
Boers had taken them?'*

Möller, meanwhile, had disappeared behind the hill. Once there,
Major E. C. Knox led a wide sweep to the east and made contact with
the enemy's tethered horses. He gave Möller the opportunity to destroy
the Boers' escape route but the latter refused to take this chance. While
Knox got back to camp that evening through Smith's Nek, Möller was
driven back round the eastern side of Impati and had to surrender at
Adelaide Farm, 8 miles north of Dundee.

The two batteries were now re-sited at Smith's Nek but though
riders could be seen fleeing, uncertainty about their identity prevented
the firing of a shot. These two failures, those of the cavalry and the

MOLLER'S
SURRENDER
4.00 pm

Sunday's River

Sand River

IMPATI

BOER ADVANCE
NIGHT OF 19th / 20th

AND RETREAT pm 20th

MOLLER
MID-DAY

1.15 pm

TALANA
HILL

8.00 am

INFANTRY

KNOX
MID-DAY

Camp

DUNDEE

LENNOX
HILL

Camp
21st Oct

5.45 am

KNOX
RETURNS
7.00 PM

Camp
22st Oct

BRITISH
RETREAT OF
22nd

TALANA HILL – 20 OCTOBER 1899

British | Boers | British | British
Cavalry | | Infantry | Artillery

artillery, spoiled all the infantry's good work.

The action, inaccurately described as at Glencoe, was reported in The Times of Saturday October 21st as though a great win. 'Latest Intelligence - British Victory - Attack on Glencoe,' said the headlines to an article datelined Ladysmith, October 19th. At one point we read, 'General Symons has been wounded. 10 a.m.' The *Manchester Guardian* was also expansive in its summary,

> 'At 1.30, the position was gained, the Boers having precipitately evacuated. What had commenced with the battle of Dundee ended in glorious victory for our arms, which must be known as the battle of Talana Hill.'

The lesser organs followed suit, and on Saturday October 21st the weekly *Barnsley Chronicle* informed its readers as quickly as did the mighty 'Thunderer', when a confident and not altogether inaccurate report was interlarded with headlines like: 'GREAT FIGHT AT GLENCOE. **DEFEAT OF THE BOERS. CAPTURE OF FIVE GUNS.**' And a few lines later, '**THE BRILLIANCE OF THE BRITISH VICTORY. HEAVY LOSS OF BRITISH OFFICERS. ENEMY HOTLY PURSUED.**'

Black and White Budget Transvaal Special wrote, 'The Transvaal Boers, under Lucas Meyer, occupied Smith's Hill, commanding our camp, and commenced missing us with their German guns and gunners. But General Symons knew his business. "Here's a chance for the Irish boys," he said to an ADC "Move up both the Fusiliers, and let the King's Royal Rifles go too, to show that Londoners are as good as any." So our artillery covered the advance with beautifully-directed shots, the Dublin and Royal Irish Fusiliers and the Kings Royal Rifles crept up the hill, the cavalry slipped round the hill to the right to prepare for the enemy's retreat, and then, just at the right moment, we swept the foe from their position and dashed them back in to Joubert's astounded arms.'

In reporting this British victory no mention was made of the surrender of the cavalry, which did not appear in the British newspapers until October 26th; for instance, *The Times* page 5, col. 1,

> 'British Officers captured. We hear from unofficial sources that the following officers whose absence had not previously been notified to us are prisoners in the enemy's hands.'

The list starts with Lieutenant Colonel Möller.

In St. James's churchyard is the sad postscript, not just to the action,

Major General Sir W Penn Symons

Penn Symons' Grave in Dundee churchyard; then and now.

but to a man's life and personality. Here are Brevet Major R. B. Blunt; Lieutenant W. M. J. Hannah; Gunner Cambrai RA; Colour-Sergeant Anderson RDF; Private J. Grotty RDF; a civilian, Mr. Tatham; and the Vicar, Gerald Chilton Baily. Was this the one who hid the Union flag until the Boers had been driven out?

But in front and alone is Major General Sir. W. Penn Symons, with a headstone 'erected by his wife in loving memory... who fell mortally

49

Newcastle Town Hall, when recaptured by British. COURTESY NATAL WITNESS

wounded at the Battle of Talana Hill October 20th 1899.'

And who died among the Boers and the looting, when his men had gone.

The reported British casualties were 51 killed, 203 wounded, 246 taken prisoner; and for the Boers the figures were understood to be approximately 30 killed, 100 wounded and 12 taken prisoner.

At 10.00 pm on Sunday 22nd October General Joubert was in force on Impati hill and had mounted a Creusot 6" gun there. General Yule had no choice but to abandon his wounded as well as food and stores, and with four days supplies loaded on carts during the night, he marched out, leaving lighted candles in the tents. So Dundee was left to the Boers who went on a spree of looting and drinking - among the prizes was Symons's code-book, and, indeed, his body, he having died of his wounds.

For a British victory, this, with hindsight, looks awfully like a beating.

1 For Rorke's Drift, take the R33 Pomeroy and Greytown road as far as Helpmekaar (37 kms), then turn left along the dirt road to and past Fugitive's Drift to the museum, a further 22 km or so. For Isandlwana leave Dundee by the R33 towards Vryheid and after 6 kms bear right on the R68 to Nqutu, 46 km, Here the R68 makes a right turn and after 16 kilometres or so, a turn to the right, another dirt road, goes to the battlefield. It is well worth the trouble but, as it is quite remote, check local conditions before leaving Dundee.

Chapter Three

ELANDSLAAGTE
21 October 1899

General Kok was last seen, briefly, cutting the rail link at Elandslaagte on the way to Ladysmith.

We noted that if following him down the line of the N11 it was necessary to turn off to the left to reach Dundee. He did not turn off, of course, but continued to advance by leaving the railway and roughly following the line now made by the N11. After visiting Talana Hill, the visitor can rejoin Kok's route by driving west on the R68 out of Dundee for 26 kilometres, bypassing Glencoe on the left. Pleasant farmland will be crossed with views of distant mountains. Rejoining the N11 facing south, the scenic quality continues.

The British were at Dundee and, in front, 62 kilometres away at Ladysmith, but here the track would be quiet and the land almost empty of white people. The farms were isolated and Kok, like Meyer on the left wing, would not be conspicuous. The ground is broken, as it was to the north, but in great green sweeps, crowned with bare scarps. To the

General Kok with the white beard and the famous Colonel Schiel at his right elbow. Schiel was an ex-Sergeant in the Prussian army and was jailer of the Jameson raiders.

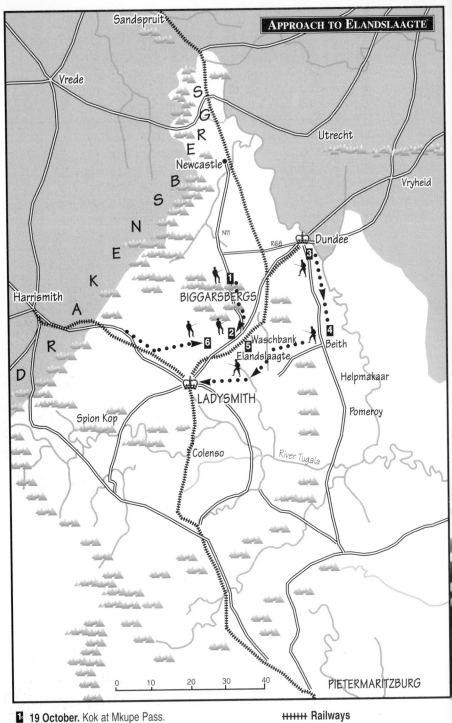

APPROACH TO ELANDSLAAGTE

Sandspruit

Vrede

Newcastle

Utrecht

Vryheid

N11

R68

Dundee

3

BIGGARSBERGS

1

Harrismith

6

2

Waschbank

5

Beith

4

Elandslaagte

Helpmakaar

LADYSMITH

Pomeroy

Spion Kop

Colenso

River Tugala

0   10   20   30   40

PIETERMARITZBURG

1 **19 October.** Kok at Mkupe Pass.
2 **19 October.** Kok at Elandslaagte.
3 **22 October.** Yule quits Dundee for Ladysmith.
4 **23 October.** Yule retreating to Ladysmith reaches Beith
5 **24 October.** Yule rests at Waschbank River.
6 **23 October.** Boers on Intitanyone.

╫╫╫╫ Railways

♛ British Garrison at Ladysmith

British   Boers

right, but thirty or so kilometres away, is the rocky Drakensberg, and now we are faced with more severely rumpled scenery in front of us. It is not a barrier like the mighty Berg to the west, but one straggling almost at right angles to that. It is the Biggarsberg range, with plenty of opportunity for hiding, either defensively or with intent to ambush.

The visitor follows Kok over Mkupe Pass, but unlike the old general he or she will find opportunities for refreshment and services on the way in this lovely area. Fort Mistake is prominent on the left of the road, perched on its own lookout hill, but, without water, not a lot of good.

We shall come to collieries, but it is hardly like the Yorks, Notts, and Derby coalfield, nor that of Lanarkshire. Maybe we could think of the South Wales mining area, not that it is similar, but at least the shape of the ground attempts to grab our attention from the winding gear and spoil heaps as it does here. To the right is Jonono's Kop, which will feature soon in the story. It must be kept in mind that the road and its traffic asserts itself now, but in 1899 the road was dwarfed by the land and only the railway had really mastered that.

J. H. M. Kok was a self-confident character, and if Joubert wanted him as his right wing, it was as a fluid operator, prepared to adopt the role of defender or marauding predator. Kok, however, either saw things differently or was carried along by his subordinates, for patrols scoured the country forward and could find no evidence of British activity apart from a supply train at Elandslaagte station. They gleefully captured it and Field-Cornet Pienaar recommended that more men be sent to the position. General Kok complied and so that night, the 18th, most of his force, including two guns, was at Elandslaagte.

J.H.M. Kok.

On the 19th, the Boers must have been well pleased with their progress. The topography favoured the advancing Meyer and Erasmus on the left, Joubert was on hand in the centre to control the push south and Kok was advancing on the right, albeit farther forward than Joubert would have liked. To complete the picture, Orange Free State's Prinsloo was down Van Reenan's Pass and pushing towards Ladysmith from the west.

The British were still strengthening themselves

53

Joubert.

significantly though, and on that day Major-General J. D. P. French arrived in Ladysmith to command the cavalry.

35 kilometres after rejoining the N11 from the R68, a turn off to the left takes the traveller to the railway, which had been coming to meet him, unseen. On its way north it serviced the pits as it found an easier route to Dundee. This junction is with the R602 and, after three kilometres, the sleepy country halt of Elandslaagte is found. French, at 8.30 am on the 20th, would have been to our right as we approach the station.

Before turning off, however, carry straight on towards Ladysmith for 7 kilometres and the Modder Spruit is reached where the British reappear in the story. The railway will have converged with the road from the left, though some distance away. Having identified the area, turn round, but exercise care, for this is a busy road, and drive back slowly.

French started briskly and went to reconnoitre the Modder Spruit the next day. In poor weather, 5th Lancers advanced the 12 miles along Dundee Road, elated, if they had heard, by news of Talana Hill and then learning from two prisoners that Elandslaagte was occupied.

On the 21st White ordered French to clear Elandslaagte and repair the railway and telegraph lines. Assigned to the task were 5 squadrons Imperial Light Horse under their commander, Colonel J. J. Scott-Chisholme, former commander of the 5th Lancers,

Major-General JDP French

Imperial Light Horse. In the centre (circled) is Scott-Chisholme, on his left Major Karri Davies and on his right Wools-Sampson.

and the Natal Field Battery of 7-pounders, all of whom went by road. Half the men of 1/Manchester Regiment entrained along with Royal Engineers' Railway and Telegraph companies. By 8.30 the men were in position a mile from Elandslaagte station facing higher ground across the road and French's cannon fired a couple of rounds, producing a response from two Boer guns. The reply was a shock and cost French an ammunition wagon so, having discovered that their firepower was greater than his was, he withdrew.

It will be worth interrupting the story to briefly comment on the Imperial Light Horse. Several irregular units were raised in the war, like the South African Light Horse, in which Churchill served, Bethune's Mounted Infantry, and Thorneycroft's Mounted Infantry, of Spion Kop fame. The ILH, however, were special for more than one reason. They had all the independence that irregulars are supposed to have, they made a name for themselves in the war for their fighting qualities, they became a permanent part of the South African Army and yet their origins were particularly offensive to the Boers.

Major C H Mullins VC

The 1895 Reform Committee in Johannesburg included ten men who eventually were the original officers of the ILH. Involved in the Jameson Raid, the product of this committee, were Colonel Frank Rhodes, Aubrey (later Sir Aubrey, KCB) Wools-Sampson, Walter 'Karri' Davies, Charles Mullins, Percy Fitzpatrick and others - several of them went to jail.

Wools-Sampson had been born in the Cape and fought alongside the Boers in the war against Sekukuni in 1878 and later was with Buller in the Zulu War of 1879. In the Boer War of 1881, he was a member of Nourses's Horse present at the siege of Pretoria. Walter Davies was an Australian engineer and came to the goldfields selling the hardwoods, Karri and Jarrah. He served in the ILH as a major for the whole of the war. Mullins, from Grahamstown, also became a major and earned the VC.

Between them all they raised sufficient money to mount and equip 1000 men, starting at the Show Grounds, Pietermaritzburg, in the first week of September. There were six squadrons of 3 troops.

Five of these squadrons were with French, which brings us back to the field of Elandslaagte.

The Boer main position was now revealed to be the ridge running

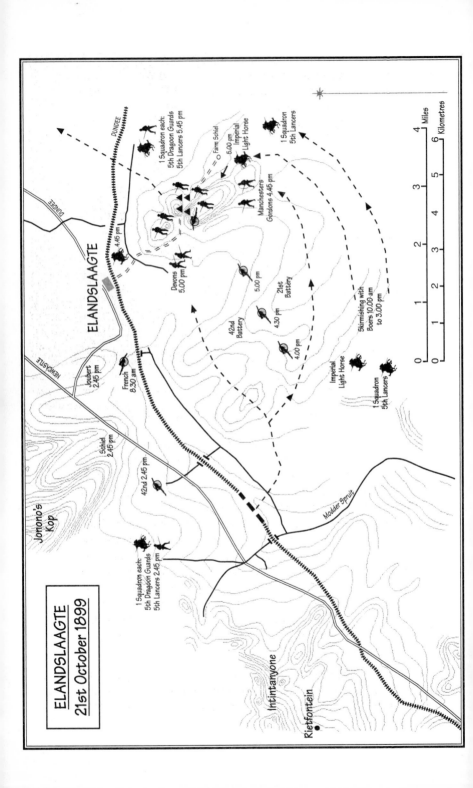

south-east from the station, starting nearest to that with an isolated kopje and beyond, another kopje, before the rest of the ridge with its flatter crown. Between this ridge and first two features was a track from the station to a farm, at the far side from French's position.

The telegraph wire was tapped, and when White learned of the Boer strength, he sent reinforcements. One squadron each of 5/Lancers and 5/Dragoon Guards with the 21st and 42nd Batteries Royal Field Artillery went by road. By rail, under the overall command of Colonel Ian Hamilton, came 1/Devons under Major Park and 5 companies of Gordon Highlanders under Lieutenant Colonel Harry Dick Cunyngham VC. French moved back to Modder Spruit and waited for their arrival.

The cavalry and artillery came by 11 o'clock, (the guns being double-

Captain P H Darbyshire, 5th Dragoon Guards who killed a Boer that had previously shot a private from under the shelter of the Red Cross flag.

teamed and at the gallop) while the Boers were half-heartedly skirmishing with ILH and 5/Lancers to the enemy's left. When these units were sent forward on French's right, determined to clear the higher ground in front of the Boer camp, Field-Cornet Pienaar fell back to the left front of the main Boer position.

Kok had with him a company of Germans holding the other flank, north of the railway line. They were commanded by the one-time Prussian Army sergeant, Colonel Schiel, and were accompanied by Field-Cornet Joubert and a hundred or so burghers. A squadron of 5/Dragoon Guards moved up to the southern tip of Jonono's Kop. They came under Maxim fire to which the 42nd Battery responded from a position west of the road to Mkupe's Pass and Newcastle *[now N11]* forcing the Germans into more broken ground, and Pienaar back to the main Boer camp.

Earlier the turnoff R602 was mentioned, (now to the right, if the visitor has turned round), and this should be taken. The ground is largely cultivated today and walkers cannot wander about at will, but consultation of the official map shows that French was to our right at 8.30am, as noted earlier.

The 5/Lancers, 5/Dragoon Guards and Natal Mounted Rifles in this area advanced across the railway, cutting the wire, but were driven back by shell fire to occupy a position near the station, ready to make the classic charge on the breaking enemy, should the chance arise.

According to the records in the possession of the Gordon Highlanders Museum at Aberdeen, this regiment received orders at 1 pm to entrain all available personnel at 1.45pm. In the event, 20 officers and 483 men found themselves on the lineside, four miles from Elandslaagte station.

By driving slowly northwards from the Modder Spruit and looking right towards the railway it will be possible to get the view that the British had as they left the train and formed up. The Imperial Light Horse and the squadron of 5/Lancers would be skirmishing with Pienaar's men away to the right as we look across the countryside. Meanwhile, two or three kilometres on to the left is where Schiel and Field Cornet Joubert were trying their luck with the Lancers and Dragoon Guards supported by the 42nd Field Battery. This was around 2.45 pm.

It was 3 pm before all the men were in position and French decided that, late as it was, he would attack. Thinking of a map as having a 'top' and a 'bottom', British troops were at the bottom, as it were, facing a patch of rather higher ground. This area stretches away to the northwest for about four miles, and, at its upper end, the railway has to skirt it eastward. In the top middle is a more level, lower area, facing the village and the coal mines, and at the back, the far wing, the ridge already described as the main camp.

Hamilton encouraged his men with the speech in which he

Elandslaagte. The kopje which was assualted by the Devons.

promised them that the newsboys in London would tomorrow morning be announcing a victory. At about 4 o'clock they moved forward. The Devons were on the left, or northern end, so would have to cross the lower area, and the Manchesters climbing over the right, with the Gordons in reserve. In the middle, the 21st and 42nd Field Batteries were placed to silence the enemy guns.

White had arrived in person and was observing from the British rear, as the Devons advanced in extended order across their bare patch in front of him, preparing to rush the higher kopje nearest the station. The Manchesters and Gordons worked round to the end of the Boer higher ground, the Gordons extending their line under heavy shellfire, with the aim of rolling the enemy up along the ridge. There were shells falling around them and the scene became floodlit by a thunderstorm beginning behind the Boers.

The Devons were advancing in extended order, which *The Times History* says was Hamilton's idea and was 'hitherto unprecedented in European warfare'. [How unlike General Hart's disastrous use of the Irish Brigade at Colenso.] In the face of heavy Mauser and artillery fire and totally exposed, but with the assistance of their extended order, the quickly failing light and the absence of red coats, they used anthills as cover. They reached the foot of their kopje by 5 pm.

On the right the Manchesters and Gordons reached the ridge and turned to the left, or north, up it to face Pienaar's retreating burghers. For about a mile, the Gordons' record says, they were directly under very heavy fire. They were joined by the dismounted ILH as they forced their way up the rough slope, and with the storm breaking, a foothold was secured on the top. The 5/Lancers, who had been in the area from the beginning, with the ILH, now took position to the south-east, ready for any Boer retreat that way.

Once on top, the men found their way barred by wire, though the volume of Boer fire poured upon them is said to have been so intense as to cut it down in many places. Obviously, however, these spots were the exception rather than the norm, and in the *The Life of a Regiment. The History of the Gordon Highlanders,* published in 1939, it is said that 'wire-cutters were not yet an issue' and numbers of desperate struggles were engaged while under the merciless fire. Lord George Murray is quoted saying,

'I find Private Fraser (the Fenian) credited with having torn the first breach with his bare hands. In another place, Denne "cut" the wire himself, while keeping his men under cover.'

By whatever means, they had to weather this storm as well as the natural elements while stumbling along the rough top. In fact, in crossing the wire the Gordon Highlanders took many casualties, including their CO, Dick Cunyngham, who sustained two wounds, and who during the action lost half his officers as casualties. In his diary, now with the Gordon Highlanders, he wrote,

> 'Regarding Elandslaagte; during the attack the Boers had orders to concentrate their fire on the Highlanders and particular squads were told off to fire only at officers.'

The commander of the 1/Manchesters, Colonel Curran, and several of his officers were likewise hurt.

As was the case throughout the war, the Boers mostly could not be seen, though Colonel Schiel was observed coming up from the farm to the east of the ridge and his Germans took heavy losses. Two curiosities here were that, besides being an ex-Sergeant in the Prussian Army, Schiel had been a jailer when the Reform Committee members were in prison, and now the Imperial Light Horse found themselves facing fellow townsmen in General Kok's Johannesburg Commando.

The advance continued in rushes with the Boers falling back and, by about 6.00 pm, the storm was at its height, illuminating the battle with forked lightening.

Hamilton came up the hill with a mixed body of men that he had collected and ordered the buglers to sound the charge. The highest end of the ridge was attacked with the bayonet and the excited men went right over its crest and down onto the Boer guns in the saddle. Captain Eric Streatfield's diary, in the Museum of the Gordon Highlanders notes,

> 'The ground sloped from the ridge to the position and down this slope the advance was conducted by short rushes, cover being taken where possible as the fire was extremely severe. Colonel Dick Cunyngham was hit in the arm about 100 yards from the fence and poor Munro shot through the head at the foot of the Boer position, he was next to me.'

The Gordon Highlanders own record states that

> 'Drum Major Lawrence with his claymore drawn was the first to reach the Bores [sic] guns and putting it down the muzzle of one he said, "I capture this gun in the name of the Gordon Highlanders."'

Their bravery was almost undone by the enemy's use of the white flag ruse, as a group of men in the laager, now exposed, made as though to surrender. Only when the soldiers moved to accept it did the Boers open fire again. General Kok was present to see the trick work and it was enhanced by a hail of bullets from the cone shaped kopje beyond the ridge. Major H. W. D. Denne, who had earlier cut the wire, fell dead beside Hamilton and many others fell dead or wounded. [H W Denne Denne had served the regiment since 1880 and was with the 1st battalion in the Egyptian campaigns of 1882/4 and 1884/5.]

The shock was so severe that the guns, newly won, were temporarily lost again and lost long enough for the Devons, slogging up the face of the last slope, to be under fire.

Captain Streatfield went on,

> I took half a company down to our right to try to get round the Boers but so many men were hit I rejoined the firing line with them again - shortly afterwards the cease fire sounded and we retired about 50 yards to a ridge of rocks, when we did this some of the Boers advanced up the reverse slope again and poured a lot of fire - Buchanan was here hit and we lost rather heavily amongst the rank and file. Meiklejohn and Sergeant Major Robertson got separated and near the Boers camp were badly wounded.'

It was temporary, though, and Hamilton again showed great bravery here. He took the lead and urged the men on, in spite of the losses, Lieutenant Meiklejohn, for instance, losing an arm. This officer was awarded the VC, along with Regimental Sergeant-Major W. Robertson, whereas Hamilton was recommended but the award was refused because of his relatively high rank. It is claimed that French himself was up among the infantrymen, urging them on. The Imperial Light Horse were particularly keen to get among the enemy and they now had extra reason when their commander, Scott-Chisholme, leading by waving his silk scarf, fell dead as the Boers attempted to recover. He was shot in the leg, then in the lungs before a bullet in his brain killed him. It is said that he died with the words, 'My fellows are doing well.' Bearing in mind that his fellows did not exist as a unit two

Scott Chrisholme's memorial.

months before, they had certainly learned a lot. Here, Captain C. H. Mullins won his VC, as did Captain R. Johnstone when, along with A. E. Brabant, they rallied the wavering British troops.

Just at this time, the Devons arrived at the crest of each of the kopjes and both wings of the attack could turn on the Boer laager. Many of the Boers surrendered but the mass made off northwards toward Newcastle, hoping to join the Newcastle road three to four miles away. The Gordon Highlanders again,

> 'On occupying the position the Boer laager was seen below lying between the two above mentioned kopjes. Boers were seen leaving it and flying in all directions, in fact a regular "sauve qui peut".'

Thus the cavalry went into action with one of the last cavalry charges being made. For millennia men on horseback have chased their enemies to slash and stick them as they fled and today the Dragoons and Lancers were on hand to the north of the rocky outcrop so as to give chase. They fell upon the retreating Boers in the failing light and the farmers' worst fears came true. The two differing styles of warfare collided. The Boers, as always, fired for as long as possible before throwing down their arms and appealing for quarter and escape from the hated cold steel now on top of them. The cavalry, on the other hand, under fire to the last second and at full gallop, carried along by their own momentum and battle madness, needing to redress the balance with the

Elandslaagte, Imperial Light Horse Memorial.

62

Mausers, were in no position to extend mercy.

As darkness set in it came on to rain and attention turned to finding the wounded out on the veld, among them the dying Kok. Fifty officers and men were reported killed and 213 wounded, while the Boers were thought to have lost sixty-seven dead, 108 wounded and upward of two hundred taken captive.

Mr. Nevinson of the *'Daily Chronicle'* wrote on the 22nd of October,

'...on the hill in the dark. In coming down, I nearly trod on the upturned white face of an old white-bearded man. He was lying quite silent, with a kind of dignity. We asked who he was. He said, "I am Kock*[sic]*, the father of Judge Kock. No, I am not the

Elandslaagte: Boer Memorial.

commandant. He is the commandant. But the old man was wrong. He himself had been in command, though instead of fighting he had read the Bible and prayed. One bullet had passed through his shoulder, another through his groin. So he lay still and read no more.'

The Gordons took back to Ladysmith 72 prisoners but the rest of the captives need not have worried too much for little interest was shown in them, some running away in the night and some being left behind in the morning. Left behind, that is, with unbelievable extravagance, for the stores and arms captured were also ignored in the rush to return to Ladysmith.

In 1908, Ian Hamilton, now General Sir, made a speech at the unveiling of the Manchester Regiment's Memorial in that city. He gave a useful, if flowery, overview of the action,

'At Elandslaagte these lads advanced over the open for a mile under a storm of shell and bullets, and turned out from their cover the most dangerous shots in the world...[they] advanced with the greatest bravery. There never was a fairer stand-up fight than Elandslaagte; there was no thought on either side of giving way; each side steeped in the most desperate endeavour - the Boers with no idea of going back, the British with no idea of stopping, but only of going forward. I remember the loud crack of the bursting shell; I remember the long shout, the strong shout, of 'Majuba' from the Gordons; I remember Chisholme, flag in hand, waving on the Imperial Light Horse; and I remember the Manchesters fixing bayonets, and then the headlong simultaneous desperate rush on to and over the guns. Then came that incident of the white flag - the hurrahs when we thought the victory was won - and then the Boers, proud men in the prime of life, aristocrats, farmers, landowners, astonished and surprised to find themselves routed, the best of them rallying, refusing defeat; no surrender, ignoring death, charging up that strong kopje. I remember our left wavering with awful hesitation, and the slow reluctant ebb of the human tide, the Boer guns abandoned, and the

example and entreaties of our officers, and the Devons pouring in on the left flank. The Manchesters advanced with a yell, and then once more that wild cry, 'Majuba,' echoing out over the darkening veldt, proclaiming the victory and honour of the Army achieved....'

The two kopjes now have the graves and memorials of Boers and soldiers, including Scott-Chisholme and while visiting these a further overview of the battlefield can be had. There is another cemetery in a nearby wood.

The next day the British people were reading Ripping Recitals of Tommy Triumphant, but, back at Dundee, General Yule was coming to understand that if he had won anything, it was but a reprieve. He moved his camp on the 21st and again on the 22nd but was still under the nose of Long Tom, the 155mm Creusot that Joubert had positioned on Impati. When the mists burned off, a 96-lb shell could be dropped on the garrison at will and on the 22nd one of them killed Lieutenant W. M. J. Hannah, of 1/Leicesters.

Civilians were taking cover as far as possible from the cannon or were leaving town altogether to go towards Ladysmith. After an

Impati viewed from Talana. Joubert's six inch gun placed up there drove Yule and the British out.

abortive attempt to occupy Glencoe Junction, Yule decided that it was time for him to go too. He acted on advice and left behind the townspeople, his tents, three months' stores and Penn Symons and the other wounded. The whole operation called for great secrecy and was successful. After dark thirty-three wagons were loaded with supplies for the journey and these made a rendezvous with the men, who marched out of camp silently at 9.30 pm, and though the Boers discovered the ruse the next morning, they chased along the railway towards Glencoe before realising their error.

The men rested in brief snatches, sleeping where they fell, wet or dry, and the four-mile column kept moving to Beith where it paused in early afternoon on the 23rd. After darkness fell at 6 o'clock, they began to ascend Van Tonder's Nek on the Waschbank road. Surely, the Boers knew where they were by now, and if they intended to ambush them, it would be here. There was no problem and the heights were secured to allow the crocodile to pass through and to arrive on level ground once

Long Tom crossing a drift. Courtesy of Soldiers of Gloucestershire Museum

more by about 3.00am. It was then a matter of arriving at and crossing the Waschbank River safely, which was accomplished as a matter of priority. The luxury of a rest in unaccustomed sunshine was enjoyed, which was as well, for after a time the rain came down in torrents again.

Study of the map shows that the Dundee contingent had to get past Elandslaagte and Sir George White's retirement from that station two days before had created a vacuum filled by Free State Boers. Sir George therefore decided to get their attention with a feint in the direction of Jonono's Kop.

While Yule was in the valley of the Waschbank, White was leaving Ladysmith with Ian Hamilton and the 1/Gloucesters, 1/Devonshires, 1/Liverpools, 2/KRRC, and Major General French commanding 5/Lancers, 19/Hussars, ILH, and a party of Natal Mounted Volunteers. The 42nd and 53rd Field Batteries along with the 10th Mountain Battery provided artillery.

They carried three days rations but never reached Jonono's Kop for they were fired on from the heights of Intintanyone to the west of the road. This led to the engagement known as Rietfontein after the farm of that name. (See maps on page 52, 56)

The historical record of the King's Liverpool Regiment is that of a

unit which was mostly employed in tedious defensive work without being involved in the major incidents like Elandslaagte and Platrand. Reading this account highlights the bouts of boring attention to detail interspersed with risk of violent death such as befell them and the Gloucesters.

After reaching the rendezvous at 5 am they were used as support to the firing line, in lines of sections at 25 pace intervals. The main body arrived at 8 am and moved up, occupying the right of the ridge facing Intintanyone with the 1/Gloucesters on the left. In the late morning the Gloucesters advanced straight at the Boer position, the reason not being known. They drew a fierce hail of bullets and seven men, including the commander, Colonel Wilford, were killed with forty men wounded. At 2 pm, when it was felt that the Dundee column was no longer threatened, the column marched back to Ladysmith. In total 14 officers and men were killed and 98 wounded with 2 missing. The Boers were reported as having 13 dead and 31 wounded.

The attention of the Boers was taken, though, and Yule's column struggled on, crossing Sunday's River midmorning, and after marching a further six miles, settling down to rest. No sooner was this done than the advance party of a column under Colonel Dartnell, sent out by White, brought the order to keep moving. They ended the retreat from Dundee in the worst possible agony, short of being molested by the enemy, marching through the night of the 25th/26th in the dark in pouring rain, unable to see a yard before their faces. The road, if road it was, was a quagmire, so that daybreak found them still seven miles away from Ladysmith, calling up their last reserves to march into Ladysmith in some sort of order.

Yule's column retreating on Ladysmith.

What of Dundee? The Boers outside eventually realized that they had been duped and they took control of the town the afternoon after the British left, the 23rd. No real attempt was made to stop General Yule but, instead, the burghers engaged in a drunken orgy of theft, to be followed as thieves, if not as drunks, by their wives.

On the 25th, even as Yule was crossing the Sunday's River, resting and then being roused for the nightmare flounder through the mud, the main body of the Boers moved down the road from Glencoe to Ladysmith. By the time the former Dundee garrison was settled in Ladysmith, the Boers had their noose half completed, the eastern and northern hills next to town being in their hands.

The Sabbath, throughout the siege, was a rest day, but the Boers interpreted their own rule as a rest from *killing*. There was no rest from the preparation for killing, and that weekend, the 28th and 29th of October, they could be seen building a gun platform on Pepworth Hill, heralding the arrival of the Creusot. Also, the town's water supply was cut off.

White's last attempt to stop the investing of the town was now to be made, on the Monday - 30th October, 'Mournful Monday.'

Chapter Four

LADYSMITH UNDER SIEGE

In the spring of 1812 in Spain, the Viscount Wellington's army concluded the difficult siege of Badajoz. When the city fell the fighting gave place to a dreadful drunken debauch as, it is said, the British soldiers were out of control. Civilians were abused and their goods stolen, and not just their chattels, for it is on record that a group of young girls were herded together to be sold off to officers.

One young officer was Harry Smith. He had joined as an Ensign in 1805 and was in the course of making a distinguished career that took him eventually to North and South America, the Caribbean and South

Boer Commando near Ladysmith. Courtesy Soldiers of Gloucestershire Museum.

Africa. Then, in India, he led the charge that won the battle of Aliwal in January 1846, making him a Baronet and Major-General. From 1847 to 1852 his career was at its zenith when he served as Governor and High Commissioner in the Cape.

But that day in Badajoz he made a decision that affected the rest of his life, for he chose Miss Juana Maria de los Dolores de Leon, aged 14. He saved her honour, though he could not save her earrings, which had been torn from her, and he married her in three days. She shared the rest of the campaign with him as Mrs. Smith, and became in due course, the Governor's Lady in the Cape Colony. When he became a Baronet, she became Lady Smith.

Ladysmith was built in a bend in the Klip River at what, in 1847, looked an easily defensible site and it became a township in 1850, taking its name from the Governor's wife. There were ripples of excitement there, like the need for a fort that was felt in 1879, but

mostly it enjoyed a life of steady growth. The climate was tolerable, land thereabouts was capable of being farmed, and, when the railway came from Durban, the junction was made here between the line to Orange Free State and that to the Transvaal. With all these advantages, there was the bonus that it was near to the coalmines being developed just to the north.

These were advantages, but in the 1890s there was still much to be done to take the town beyond potential to actual prosperity, and with the limitations of Victorian technology it was still a dusty, pestilential place with functional steel-roofed bungalows. A snatch of mordant poetry penned by Robert King in 1899 is displayed in the Siege Museum:

'Ladysmith thou art supremely cussed
with flies, bad water and with dust.
A filthy fever-stricken nest
with no redeeming feature blest.'

Murchinson Street on 'Mournful Monday.' COURTESY OF 'NATAL WITNESS'.

The famous photograph of the British Army crowding along Murchison Street on 30th October 1899 supports this picture. It is viewed through a haze of dust, which in wet weather would be the composition of the street's quagmire.

As it turned out the defensive capability was never tested until October 30th 1899, when the town had already developed into a vast stores and training camp. With the appearance of the Naval Brigade and the disappearance of the last trains for the south on November 2nd, such a test began.

There for examination were the following:

    5/Lancers.
    5/Dragoon Guards.
    19/Hussars.
    21st, 42nd and 53rd batteries Royal Field Artillery.
    10th Mountain Battery.
    1/Manchesters.
    1/Liverpools and one company of Mounted Infantry.
    1/Devonshires.
    2/King's Royal Rifles.

The same view today.

2/Gordon Highlanders.
1/Gloucesters.
2/Rifle Brigade.
Royal Engineers; 23rd Field Company as well as telegraph and balloon sections.
Natal Mounted Rifles, approximately 1200 men.
Natal Carbineers.
Border Mounted Rifles.
Natal Police.
Natal Naval Volunteers.
Imperial Light Horse.
Naval Brigade.
General Yule augmented the garrison with, from Dundee,
1/Royal Irish Fusiliers.
1/Leicesters.
1/King's Royal Rifles.
2/Dublin Fusiliers.
18/Hussars.
13th, 67th and 69th batteries Royal Field Artillery.

The 1/King's Liverpool Regiment was among the first to arrive. They had come to South Africa from the West Indies in 1897 and now arrived in Ladysmith on 15th June 1899 to strengthen the Natal garrison. At first they camped southeast of town on the bank of the Klip River, but after six weeks they moved to a position east of Tin

A parade before the siege began. The Town Hall is visible and the building in front of it is now part of the Siege Museum. The great open area, the cricket field, is now the Oval Shopping Precinct.

SEIGE MUSEUM

OVAL SHOPPING PRECINCT

Camp and south of King's Post, being inspected on the 22nd by General Penn Symons.

The last to arrive was the Naval Brigade, just before the Boers shut the gate, and they made all the difference. There were 283 officers and men under Captain Hedworth Lambton, with two 4.7" and three long 12-pounders on Captain Percy Scott's carriages, one 12-pounder 8cwt gun and four Maxims, one of which was tripod mounted and three on wheels.

12,500 officers and men were locked up along with 5,400 civilians and 2,400 Blacks and Indians, who, presumably, did not count either as servicemen or as civilians to the one who prepared the list. Another interesting statistic is that there was 'enough food for two months, and only one month's food for the 10,000 horses and 2,500 oxen.' In view of Baden Powell's appalling dishonesty in Mafeking, this begs the question, 'who has done the counting?'

Had it struck anybody before that these meadows were overlooked on every side? Certainly, Buller had counselled that the British should not be caught north of the River Tugela, but here they were in full view of a circle of kopjes. Rifleman's Ridge, Star Hill, Telegraph Ridge to the west; Surprise Hill, Bell's Kop, Pepworth Hill, Limit Hill to the north; Gun Hill, Lombard's Kop, and the mighty Umbulwana to the east, all were controlled by the Boers. To the south was the long hill which the Boers knew as Platrand, and the British called Wagon Hill at its western end, and Caesar's Camp at its eastern - fortunately this was 'ours'. Sir Archibald Hunter said Ladysmith was in the bottom of a teacup, which was similar to, if more polite than, the French officer's description of Dundee.

The British had their own high points within the trap. In a clockwise direction Signpost, Range Post and Ration Post westward, King's Post, Observation Hill, Gordon Hill and Junction Hill to the north, the Helpmekaar Ridge to the east and the Platrand just mentioned. The dominating high ground, though, was in the invaders' hands.

Ladysmith has grown, of course, since 27th February 1900, but the town that Sir George White knew is recognisable because it is half-contained in the bend in the Klip River, a girdle at once protective and threatening. The original defensive position had already persuaded the town to grow northeastwards in those days, with Murchison Street the main shaft. This is still the centre of affairs.

Since White's time, though, the area bounded by the inner ring of hills has been filled with a series of residential sections, but this should not put the battlefield visitor off. All the features of the story are easily

Looking over Murchison towards the Platrand.

The Royal Hotel. The view on page 72 must have been taken from the far end of the balcony. Dr Stark (page 92) was killed to the right of were the horse is standing.

found and recognizable.

The visitor is strongly advised to go to the Siege Museum first and soak up the presentations there before getting a copy of the 'Guide to Historic Ladysmith' with its walkabout map.

To start at the bottom of Murchison Street, with back to town, where the river obliged the planners to make a 'T' junction; one may look at the right turn, or westwards. This is onto the N11, directing the visitor, after 7 km, at another left on R103 to Colenso, or, ignoring that, for another 8 km, to a further left (R600) for the Spion Kop 'round'.

King's Post at the North West corner of the defences (see page 82).

From Observation Hill.

Directions are found in 'Relief of Ladysmith', this volume's companion book.

Studying the modern town map in clockwise fashion and starting at the N11, the district of Van Riebeeck Park on the steep southern bank of the Klip River is seen first. This area was at the extreme western end of Section 'C', Hamilton's responsibility, and west of it are the high points known as Range Post and Rifleman's Post.

Across the river is Hospital Park on the road out past the Army Depot and the site of Tin Camp. This is the R103 leading to N3 and Van Reenan's Pass. To the left is a good view of Spion Kop in the distance, and it is out on this road, to the right, that McMasters' Blockhouse is to be

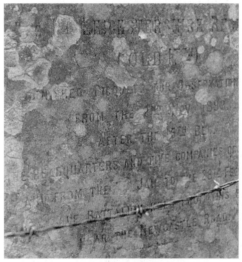

The badly weathered stone shown above reads: '...Leicester Regiment (Old 17th) ...picquet for Observation Hill from the 2nd November 1899. After the 15th December the Headquarters and five companies occupied and from....Jan to the 28th Feb 1900 whole of Battalion held from this point to near the Newcastle Road.' (See page 82)

found. This is a privately built and owned replica of a British Blockhouse with a wealth of Boer and Zulu War artefacts. Viewing is by appointment and arranged at the Siege Museum.

Moving clockwise on the map we are now in General Howard's sector, Section 'B'. King's Post and Cove Redoubt, the home of the 4.7" called 'Princess Victoria', are in the area now known as Reservoir Hill, which faces the golf course and even sports a road named 'Chevril'. Observation Hill is developed and has kept its name, where we can find the badly weathered Leicester Memorial. From here are views of Boer territory; notably Surprise Hill and, further away Tchrengula where the debacle at Nicholson's Nek occurred. At our back, towards town, is Gordon Hill with the Dragoon Guards Monument, before we arc round further to the district known as Egerton and the site of the Lady Anne Battery.

We are now looking at Section 'A', where Colonel Knox was in charge and, beyond the railway line, the housing developments are generally less plush than those just described. Here were the Devons and the Liverpools and the KRRC, on the higher ground of Tunnel and Cemetery Hills and Helpmekaar Ridge.

The line completes by crossing the meadowland beside the Klip and across to the foot of Caesar's Camp and back to Colonel Ian Hamilton.

How the war would have turned out if General Joubert had raced for the sea and a port of his own at Durban, it cannot be said, but it is now generally reckoned that the sieges of Mafeking, Kimberley and

The first British response. One of the elderly howitzers, 'Castor' and 'Pollux'.

Ladysmith were not worth the expense of resources of men and time.

But here he was with the big guns that caused the biggest commotion in the story. It seems strange that even in this war when there were so many uses and abuses of the conventions of chivalry, the Dutch found the shelling of civilians to be acceptable. But then, later in the war, the British hierarchy did not believe that conditions in Concentration Camps were as terrible as they had allowed them to be.

Three 155mm Creusot guns were brought down from Pretoria and placed on Pepworth Hill, Umbulwana and Telegraph Hill from where they dropped their deadly missiles on the town. Long Tom is the famous one, but is actually the shortest lived, as we shall see. Puffing Billy on Umbulwana and Fiddling Jimmy on Telegraph Hill were the most dangerous.

The British would have been lost for a reply without the navy's contribution. They had the two old Howitzers brought up from Cape Colony, as well as the Field Artillery and the Mountain battery, but all were well outraged by the Creusots. The naval guns were available thanks to Captain Scott RN of HMS *Terrible* who, as lately as October 21st, had his 12-pounders removed from the decking and mounted on timber frames with wagon wheels. Sir George White knew that his artillery was no match for the Creusots, and at the suggestion of Sir Henry Rawlinson, he appealed for help to Rear-Admiral Sir Robert Harris, Commander in Chief, Cape of Good Hope and West Africa Station. His Captain Scott was ready. The garrison in Ladysmith and the Relief Force had some sort of answer to the Cruesots and the Krupps.

Cooped with Sir George White were other note-worthy figures, including some of those who had done time for their part in the Jameson Raid. Colonel Frank Rhodes DSO was there, along with Lieutenant Colonel A. Wools-Sampson, Major W. 'Karri' Davies and the arch-plotter himself, Dr. Leander Starr Jameson. The Boers were particularly keen to shell him.

Others would be remembered too, some in a limited way, and not all soldiers. 'Scribblers' were very busy. There were newspapermen like George Steevens of the 'Daily Mail' and W. T. Maud, artist of the 'Graphic', Nevinson of the 'Daily Chronicle'

Dr Leander Starr Jameson.

Gordon Highlanders camp.

and H.H.S. Pearse, the 'Daily News' special correspondent. Amateurs, male and female, like Bella Craw, confided the day's experiences to paper or writing letters when this was possible. Soldiers made or added to the lustre of long careers - or detracted from it; and they wrote too. George White himself, Harry Dick Cunyngham, Lieutenant Colonel C. W. Park of the 1/Devonshire Regiment, Captain Steavenson of the Liverpools' Mounted Infantry, or Sergeant-Major Walter Shaw.

Sir Archibald Hunter should have been Buller's Chief of Staff but found himself trapped with General White, as did Sir Henry Rawlinson, who was on his way to high honours.

Johnny Gough had what must have been an emotional meeting with his brother Hubert Gough of the Relief Column on the evening when Buller's mounted troops eventually broke through in February. Then there were the six who won VCs; Privates Scott and Pitts, Lancashire lads of the 1/Manchester Regiment; Trooper Albrecht, Imperial Light Horse; Lieutenant Digby-Jones, Royal Engineers; Lieutenant Norwood, 5/Dragoon Guards; and Lieutenant James Masterson, 1/Devonshire Regiment.

As October proceeded, the garrison expanded very quickly, the 2/Gordon Highlanders coming into town at 3.00 am on the 10th and marching up to Tin Camp, where they were when the Boers declared war on the 12th. Their commander, Lieutenant Colonel William Henry 'Harry' Dick Cunyngham, had joined up in 1872 and was in the Afghan War of 1878-80 when he won the VC on the road to Kandahar - and he had less than three months left to live. Mr. Nevinson had written on the 11th, seemingly inaccurately, 'the only line battalion present is the Liverpools', but he continued with greater truth...' Ladysmith has an evil reputation besides. Last year the troops here were prostrated with enteric. There is a little fever and a good deal of dysentery even now among the regulars. The stream by the camp is condemned and all water is supplied in tiny rations from pumps. Half of the Manchesters have just marched in.'

The 1/Irish Fusiliers arrived in railway trucks in 'the wet early morning' of October 13th, five companies being assigned to immediate outpost duty and the other three marching off to Tin Camp.

If the water and the flies were bad for the newcomers, they did not yet have boredom to contend with. On the same day that the Irish Fusiliers arrived, the Gordons were sent out west 12 miles towards Van Reenan's Pass to cut off 3000 Boers and 18 guns, but none were to be found.

The 1/Gloucesters came in by train from Durban and the boat early on the 14th, shortly to face their first action since the Indian Mutiny, at Rietfontein.

The Irish Fusiliers suddenly moved out again - on the night of the 15th by the Dundee train, to a date at Talana Hill.

On the 18th the Gordons flitted again in what they called 'The flight from Tinville', making a bivouac south of Gordon Post, with 'D' company marching next day to Cove Redoubt and 'F' company to Gordon Post.

There was plenty of work for this battalion and on the 20th there began the activities described in the previous chapter.

On the 26th, at 2.00pm, the Irish Fusiliers marched back into Ladysmith from Dundee, soaked and covered in mud. Here they found themselves brigaded with the Manchesters, the Devons and the Gordons under Ian Hamilton.

On the 29th, they were back at Tinville again in time to form part of that fated column that included the Gloucesters and No 10 Mountain Battery, commanded by their own commander, Lieutenant Colonel Carleton. They were to make a night march northwards to attack the Boers, while the main force probed out to the east in the direction of Helpmekaar.

We have now rejoined the chronology of the story which we left temporarily at the end of the last chapter and the biggest disaster of the whole episode was about to befall the garrison the next day, 'Mournful Monday', 30th October. Colonel Grimwood was defeated at Lombard's Kop, partly due to the failure of John French's cavalry on his right.

The 1/Liverpools was part of his Brigade and its role was a share with 2/King's Royal Rifle Corps, 1/Gloucesters and 2/Dublin Fusiliers in the attack on Long Hill. When in position south of the hill they found themselves under attack from 'many guns and many MI from beyond the Modder Spruit.' The enemy tried to turn both British flanks

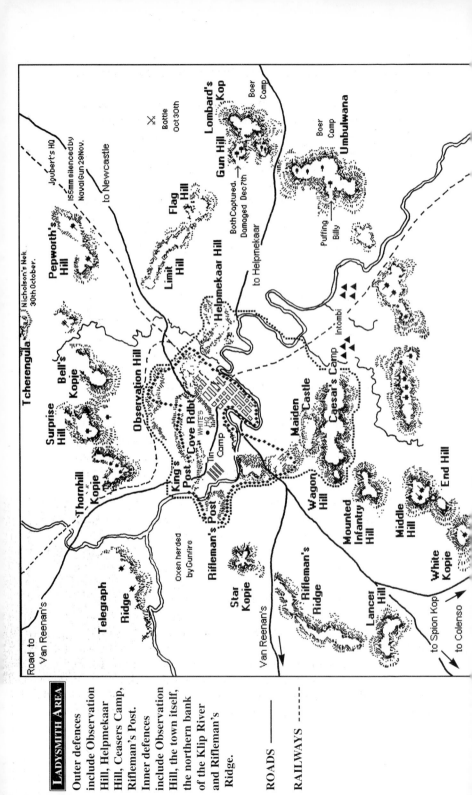

LADYSMITH AREA

Outer defences include Observation Hill, Helpmekaar Hill, Ceasers Camp, Rifleman's Post. Inner defences include Observation Hill, the town itself, the northern bank of the Klip River and Rifleman's Ridge.

ROADS ——

RAILWAYS ------

Road to Van Reenen's

Nicholson's Nek. 30th October.

Tchetengula

Joubert's HQ

155mm silenced by Naval Gun 29 Nov.

to Newcastle

Battle Oct 30th

Lombard's Kop

Boer Camp

Gun Hill

Both Captured. Damaged Dec 7th

Boer Camp

Umbulwana

Puffing Billy

to Helpmekaar

Flag Hill

Pepworth's Hill

Limit Hill

Surprise Hill

Bell's Kopie

Helpmekaar Hill

Thornhill Kopie

Observation Hill

Intombi

King's Post

Cove Rdbt

WHITE'S HQ

Tin Camp

Maiden Castle

Caesar's Camp

Oxen herded by Gunfire

Rifleman's Post

Telegraph Ridge

Star Kopie

Wagon Hill

Mounted Infantry Hill

Rifleman's Ridge

Middle Hill

End Hill

Van Reenan's

Lancer Hill

White Kopie

to Spion Kop

to Colenso

so the brigade had to turn to face right front in a battle that lasted from 5 am to 3 pm.

Some enemy shells fell near the Liverpools' Maxim gun, causing the mules to break away from the man holding them. They careered towards the enemy until, when a wheel struck an anthill, one mule escaped and the other fell over. Lieutenant Watt and 4938 Private Kemp with three others of the maxim detachment righted the gun and dragged it to cover.

All this attracted heavy fire from Pepworth and Long Hills and a shrapnel shell burst in front of the gun, scoring the ground and carriage but wounding no one. The battalion covered the brigade's retirement under heavy fire, with the Devons, remaining on rising ground above Ladysmith, being the last battalion to leave.

The action was a festival of mules, it seems because *The History of The 17th (The Leicestershire Regiment)* page 210 says,

> 'the battalion was part of the 8th Brigade when it became engaged in the action at Lombard's Kop....4 mules of the mountain gun ran away, and under heavy fire from all kinds of projectiles, the gun had to be abandoned. Having attempted to recover it, Corporals Gillespie and Harris were awarded the DCM.'

Another decoration from this day's work was the VC awarded to Second Lieutenant John Norwood, whose patrol was driven back by heavy fire. This officer returned, picked up a wounded trooper and set him upon his horse. He walked and led the horse home, all the time under heavy fire.

Act Three of the Mule's Ballet was danced in the northern sortie, which turned into an utter tragedy. Colonel Carleton suffered a fate worse than death at Nicholson's Nek.

With six companies of the Gloucesters and 4 guns of No. 10 Mountain Battery, the Irish Fusiliers marched for over two hours and then turned left up a steep, rocky hill. Half way up there was an alarm at the head of the column and the ammunition mules stampeded and ran through the men and away. When they did reach the top of the hill, at its northern end, they moved southwards along it and the Gloucesters were deployed to defend the western slope, while the Irish Fusiliers defended the eastern slope. The

Second Lieutenant J Norwood VC.

83

mountain battery was now rendered useless, of course. At daylight, the enemy began to fire upon them from their rear and men began to fall. The Boers were invisible and continued to inflict casualties upon the British until 2.00 pm when it was obvious that they were surrounded and under fire from every direction save south. They were fixing bayonets when, says Captain Burrowes, 'we heard shouts that the cease-fire had sounded but thinking it was a Boer ruse we continued to fire until ordered to lay down our arms; which order came as a complete surprise and shock.' The Regimental History[1] (p255) says,

> 'It is pointless after this lapse of time to speculate on the sad questions of how and when and by whom the white flag was displayed. No Irish Fusilier who was present at this unfortunate battle, whatever his rank, will admit that it was an officer or man of the Regiment. What is certain is that a little group of British soldiers did show that flag. As the men near him had no more ammunition, Carleton acquiesced; for he had seen the main Ladysmith force retire after an unsuccessful engagement, making no move to help him, beyond signalling him to withdraw when he was already cut off. Since his heliograph was on a runaway mule, Carleton could not even reply to this message or appeal for assistance.'

So, 13 officers and 480 men from the Irish Fusiliers joined Möller and his 18/Hussars in captivity in Pretoria, and Carleton presided over the surrender of 954 men in all. Joubert himself is said to have effectively

Naval 12 pounder on Captain Scott's wooden frame and cart wheels.

rescued the British by failing to follow the disorganised mob that was left, and destroying it. He said, it seems, 'When God extends a finger, you do not take the hand.' Botha, De Wet, De la Rey and the others would have; and the arm as well.

The British suffered 69 killed and 339 wounded besides the 954 missing. The naval 12-pounders expended 25 shells and the soldiers' .303s fired 422,247 rounds.

The navy, arriving in Ladysmith at 8.30am, had been brought into the fray immediately in front of Limit Hill. At the end of the twentieth century, 'immediately' looks to be a relative term, if that is possible. Urging, harnessing and driving the fifty spans of oxen that were used to pull the 12 pounders out to Limit Hill sounds anything but fast, and before they could get into position they were recalled. While falling back again they were shelled by the Creusot on Pepworth Hill and the leading 12- pounder was overturned, its oxen scattering, mule-fashion. The other two guns were used to silence the bigger Boer gun and allow the withdrawal to continue. The upset gun was later recovered.

At Newarke Houses in Leicester is the diary of Private Arthur Nicholls of 1/Leicesters. He had joined on 21st July 1892, aged 18 years 3 months, at that time in "E" Company. Private Nicholls' company was not in the battle on the 29th it appears, but on the 31st he records,

> 'We came across some of the remains of yesterday's fight, one field gun that had been captured off the enemy and afterwards used by our men, with their wheels smashed up [sic]... tins of marmalade, empty ginger beer bottles. Breakfasted on coffee, bread and bully beef. 3 killed and 28 wounded.
>
> Several men are missing from different Regiments, 100 men of the 11th Hussars and a battalion of rifles also 2 of the Hotchkiss guns which fire Lyddite, also big guns from off the "Terrible" and poorly manned by Blue Jackets [sic].'

This last comment is interesting for, if Private Nicholls is referring to the long 12-pounder overturned, it has become plural. Also, he seems to have the same poor view of naval gunnery as that expressed later by Sir Archibald Hunter to the members of the Commission which enquired into the War in South Africa in 1902-03. This officer said, 'Our gun-laying in the Army is infinitely better than the gun-laying in the Navy... Navy in Ladysmith left a lot to be desired. Practice made by the 4.7s was - I do not want to use too harsh a term - well it was such that I offered to take the girls out of school

85

Captain Hedworth Lambton

CIRCULAR MEMO., No. 393 A.

DEFENCES OF LADYSMITH.

To the Officers Commanding Sub-Sections of the Defences of Ladysmith.

All the Defensive posts must be strengthened to the utmost. The C.R.E. will detail an R.E. Officer to supervise each sub-section. The works will be improved and extended, if necessary, by the Garrisons of the Posts, and supports, under the direction of the R.E. Officer.

Definite orders must be *written* out for the O.C. of each post by Commanders of sections, to be handed over from one O.C. post to another, on relief.

These orders must show :—

1. The extent of the ground to be occupied by the post.

2. The direction from which danger is most likely to be apprehended.

3. The position of the supports and reserves.

4. The position of the reserve ammunition.

5. The position of the rations, water, &c.

6. To whom to send, and where to send, if further reinforcements of men are required, or if extra ammunition is wanted.

7. That signalling arrangements between posts and Headquarters Camp will be arranged by the Divisional Signalling Officer.

8. Arrangements for communicating with supports and reserves.

9. To whom reports should be made of any movements of the enemy observed from the post.

Arrangements should be made for storing each post with ammunition. There should not be less in each post, including that carried by the soldier, than 300 rounds per rifle for a full garrison.

This reserve ammunition must be placed in a convenient and protected position in the immediate vicinity of the post; the R.E. Officer will arrange for the efficient protection of this ammunition.

A tank must be placed in each post to contain sufficient water for a two days supply for a full garrison. Arrangements should be taken to protect these tanks, both from rifle fire and the sun.

A two days supply of rations and firewood must be stored for a full garrison in the vicinity of each post. These rations and wood must only be used on an emergency.

Schemes must be drawn up giving the strength of the supports and reserves for each post, also positions to be taken up by these bodies. These troops should parade *daily at 4.30 a.m.*, and should remain on their parades until 5.30 a.m., when, if not required, they can be dismissed by their respective Commanding Officers.

Each officer in charge of a post will be provided with a plan showing the defences of Ladysmith. This will be passed on from one commanding officer of a post to another, on relief; the ranges of all important points should be entered on these plans.

Hours for the relief of posts to be fixed.

These orders to be issued at once, copies of the same, together with all information called for in this Circular, to be submitted to the Chief Staff Officer with the least possible delay.

By Order

A. HUNTER, *Major-General.*
CHIEF STAFF OFFICER NATAL FIELD FORCE.

Head Quaters, Natal Field Force, Ladysmith, 31st October, 1899.

to come and serve.'

That led, of course to a tart response from Captain Hedworth Lambton, 'He shows himself to be an extremely ignorant man. He is a very gallant man, but it is bravery and stupidity combined in his case.'

It was after Mournful Monday that the ring was complete and the defences were allocated into sectors along a 14-mile perimeter, enclosing an area with a diameter of some four miles. There were telephone communications to the veranda at White's HQ, 16 Poort Road.

All the *alarums and excursions off* were now over, apart from the occasional night sorties and, generally, the various regiments became associated with geographical points.

The Liverpools, for instance, were transferred on the 31st October to 8 Brigade under Colonel W. G. Knox and were moved to a camp near the railway. According to the diary of Captain Steavenson, commanding the regiment's Mounted Infantry, they took over the camp of the Gloucesters who had been captured at Nicholson's Nek. The work was defensive, of course, and Sir Archibald Hunter's evidence to the War Commission (Vol II) said,

Major-General Sir Archibald Hunter KCB DSO. White's Chief of Staff.

> "The most difficult defence, by far, to hold because it was the most dominated - it being lowest - was Colonel William Knox's. It was a mass of low-lying hills frowned upon from the heights of Bulwana and Lombard's Kop and, from their superior position, the long-range guns of the enemy could point down upon the top of Colonel William Knox. He built up enormous stone traverses, capable of resisting any shell fire we have ever seen yet."

He was known to his men as 'Nasty Knox'...

These positions included four defensive posts, Liverpool Castle and Tunnel Hill facing North, with Cemetery Hill and Helpmekaar, or Devon Post, facing east towards Lombard's and Umbulwana.

A routine was quickly adopted by both sides and, in spite of having to cope with the shelling, there must have been long boring passages for both sides. Life was for the besieged made the plainer by rationing - but, for besieged and besieger alike, spiced by disease. The soldier's day could start at 3.15 am when he paraded, before sleeping again with his kit on until another parade at 6 am. Drill, running and PT were followed by breakfast at 7.30. He could then expect fatigues, possibly guard duty and a rifle inspection before dinner. The afternoon might

A memorandum from Headquarters.
COURTESY OF THE SOLDIERS OF GLOUCESTER MUSEUM.

This Naval Gun shield marks the site of the 'Lady Anne Battery' occupied by guns of HMS Powerful during the Siege of Ladysmith. November 1899 to February 1900. It was here that Lieutenant F. Egerton RN, after whom this suburb is named, fell in action on 2 November 1899. He died, but was promoted Commander posthumously.

well be spent sleeping before the evening parade at 6 pm. Last Post was at 7.30 and Lights Out at 7.45 pm. The round went on and on, punctuated by the threat to life posed by shelling, sorties, or assaults.

Then there was still the ceaseless toing and froing to cope with, at the whim of 'them in charge'. In the case of the Liverpools, "all officers and men saw the sun rise every morning of the one hundred and eighteen days siege". No doubt many other units could say the same.

Lieutenant Michael Hodges was given command of a Naval 4.7" mounted on Junction Hill between Cove Redoubt and Tunnel Hill on 2 November. A 12-pounder Naval field gun was set up on Gordon Hill (it later moved to Junction Hill) along with the Naval Maxim Gun. One of Captain Scott's famous mutant 12-pounders was placed on Gordon Hill too, before one moved to Cove Redoubt on 22 November and one to Caesar's Camp on 27 November.

Sadly, that very first morning of the 2nd the Navy suffered a noteworthy loss through shelling. Accurate fire from Long Tom began to hamper the setting up of what became known as 'Lady Anne Battery' and, after a response from the 4.7", Lieutenant F. G. Egerton was struck by a shell. He was a nephew of the Duke of Devonshire and son of Admiral the Hon. Francis Egerton. When hit he remarked, 'this will put a stop to my cricket, I'm afraid'. He died within the hour, and is commemorated by the area, now developed residentially, being known by his name.

The view had by the men operating the Lady Anne Battery is now obscured by a private house on the lip of the hill, but the actual site is marked in front of this house's garden and is worth a visit. There is a gun-shield, which the 4.7 did not have, and a plaque with the words,

'This Naval Gun Shield marks the site of the "Lady Anne Battery" occupied by guns of HMS Powerful during the siege of Ladysmith. It was here that Commander F. Egerton RN, after whom this suburb is named, fell in action 2/11/99'

The 4.7s were now connected by telephone to the Navy's control tower on Gordon Hill and to White's HQ.

The next day, the 3rd, the Boers had a fault with their gun, which had been in action in the morning, so they flew a white flag. Incredibly, the British obliged them by ceasing fire too to let them effect repairs. However, some practical steps were taken, as when White established

Cove Redoubt and 4.7″ Naval Gun.

Ladysmith Town Hall with shell damage. See page 72 and 78.

a mobile column on half-hour stand-by with three days' supplies. Also, General Brocklehurst moved out to reconnoitre Lancers' Hill but Heilbron Commando drove him back with five killed, one missing and 28 wounded.

It was soon evident that grave problems were to come if the siege was protracted, because on 4 November an armistice was arranged when White asked Joubert to allow the transfer to the south of all civilians and sick. Joubert, from his camp 5 miles north-east of Ladysmith, turned White down, but did allow a neutral camp to be set up at Intombi, with a train going back and forth daily. The wounded, and any civilians who wished could be moved, the latter provided that they had not been involved in fighting. Joubert stipulated that he be informed of the

numbers of any such civilians.

It was now the first Sunday of the siege and the Boers had a rest day from trying to kill - but not from preparing to kill.

The extensive social life of Ladysmith-under-Siege, shelling or no shelling, had Captain Hedworth Lambton as one of its leaders and this evening, according to Dick Cunyngham's diary, the gregarious sea captain came to see him as he convalesced.

This was also the day for moving the sick to Intombi, with everything completed in 24 hours. Unfortunately it was a very windy and rainy night and the transfer was not completed. In fact, two of the sick were left on the train by mistake, and Trooper Guthrie-Smith of the Imperial Light Horse, who had been wounded at Elandslaagte, fell off his stretcher when a pole broke, which led to a setback in his condition. He died and his grave can be seen in the graveyard at Intombi.

At the start there were 300 sick being nursed by some 30 doctors and 120 trained staff. Most of them were wounded from Elandslaagte, Nicholson's Nek and Rietfontein, but the numbers of sick would keep climbing, disproportionately to the wounded, as enteric and dysentery set in. (See the map on page 82).

Imperial Light Horse Camp.
COURTESY OF 'NATAL WITNESS'

Intombi is worth a visit, though the only things there are the great Blue Gum Trees and the gravestones. Still, Umbulwana broods above the visitor and the discomfort suffered by the inmates, over and above the filth and the insects and the fever, is easily imagined. With all that, there were 155mm shells whining over their heads on the way to wreck the town beyond us.

However, let the approach be a warning. After crossing the Shepstone Bridge, go to Circle Road, a place of industry and storage which is lonely in the evenings and at weekends. Cross the railway line and turn onto the Railway Maintenance Road, as it is called. In fact, the railway may be

91

looked after, but the road isn't, being a very bad, and increasingly worse, track. Littered with rubbish, seriously rutted and the dump for industrial and fly-tipping, there are places where, in an emergency, it would be difficult to turn. It is not a trip to make alone.

At this time, bread had reached 1/- per pound and butter 3/9d per pound, with Government tobacco at 1/4d per pound.

On the Thursday the 9th November the Boers commenced shelling at 5am as a prelude to attacks from three directions. The 5/Lancers and two companies of the KRRC at Observation Hill were under heavy fire from the Pretoria Commando, advancing from Bell's Kop, while the Manchesters, Imperial Light Horse and the 42nd Battery RFA repulsed an attack on Caesar's Camp by Vryheid burghers. Later the Boers opposite Helpmekaar Ridge appeared to be attacking the positions of the Devons and the Liverpools. As if there was not enough noise, a 21-gun salute was fired at noon to celebrate the Prince of Wales's birthday and for light relief, during the day, the Boers asked the British for some chlorodyne to treat dysentery - and were supplied.

Life was dominated daily by shelling, sickness and starvation, the two former were less selective than the last in the sense that pure chance or ignorance picked you out to be shelled or contaminated, whereas wealth or sharp thinking could side-step the apocalyptic black horseman. Even General Sir George White was shelled out of his HQ with a hit that could have changed the course of the Great War. Sir Henry Rawlinson, White's ADC, had just got up from his chair when the missile destroyed it, chance saving him for future fame and a Barony. It was kind to him, but grossly unfair to Dr. A. C. Stark, for on November 18th this Devonian doctor of medicine and ornithologist was singled out, unknowingly, by one of the big guns. It was Puffing Billy on Umbulwana, according to the *Guide to Historic Ladysmith,*

Ladysmith defenders.

General White's HQ at 16 Poort Road...

...here seen after being
shelled...

...and as it is today,
smart private offices.

93

but Long Tom on Lombard's Kop according to the Siege Museum. Whichever gun released it, the shell passed through the floor of Stark's bedroom at the Royal Hotel, and went into the hall below before passing out into the street. The doctor was outside and here it removed one of the doctor's legs and smashed the other. He quickly died and a brass plate in the pavement marks the spot.

The Liverpools' records show that on 9 November Sergeant McDonnell and Private Doolan were killed at Tunnel Hill, and on the 24th a 6" shell from Umbulwana landed in the guard tent where three out of eight were thrown up in the air and slightly wounded. During the day four were killed and seven wounded. (In the next month, December, the only casualties were two men wounded.)

All the dangers were grist for the writer's mill. Typical was a letter from Sergeant-Major Walter Shaw to his cousin. He began it on November 16th and commented on the events of Mournful Monday. He then said,

> 'I have had several narrow escapes, one day a shell burst near my tent, several pieces were blown through the tent, and my kit-bag and carbine were .... smashed up, I had not left the tent many minutes when this occurred. We are anxiously looking forward to the time when the relieving force will come, though we have defended the place by throwing up earthworks, etc., and we have enough rations to keep us going for months yet, so that it would be almost impossible for the Boers to take it. At the same time, it is not very pleasant to have shells flying about you all hours of the day.'

Elsewhere on 16 November the Gordon Highlanders played the Border Mounted Rifles at football and a shell passed close overhead, falling among tents without hurting anyone. The game went on and instead of continuing the shelling, numbers of the enemy were seen standing on their parapet watching the match. (Other diversions could include a dip in the Klip in lieu of a bath, although the citizenry objected to companies of soldiers naked in the foaming billows. Did they expect men on active service to pack costumes?)

However, those in Ladysmith were relieved by the Boer's stolid attention to his own habits. Besides abstinence from serving his guns on Sundays, he liked to be in bed at night, to stop for lunch and to take an afternoon rest. On plenty of days that summer the artillery, like the cricket, was rained off, but it seems that when cricket was played, as when the Gordons beat a Ladysmith XI by seven runs, the enemy

Mr Parbhusingh awaits Puffing Billy.

restrained himself again.

There is a note on the experience of living under the threat of the 155mm Creusot in *The Life of a Regiment - The History of the Gordon Highlanders*. On page 39, presumably referring to Puffing Billy, it says,

> 'When Bulwana Tom was elevated for a shot at us, she looked like a perfect vertical chimney; when white smoke spouted from this, the watcher blew his whistle, shouted "She's off", and all took cover in the company trenches. There were 23 seconds between smoke and burst.'

That was how they experienced it in the Gordons, but others also had the assistance of Mr. Parbhusingh, described as a coolie, who stood in a dangerous and exposed position near the Commissariat watching for the gun's movements. He was prominent because of his large umbrella and the more so as he bravely waved his flag to warn of Puffing Billy's discharge.

This gentleman reminds us of the role played by the Indian community in the Boer War. He was only a labourer but was swept up with all the others into resisting the invaders. M. K. Ghandi is quite a different matter, for he was an educated man, not to be swept up. He was also disillusioned, however, and his sympathies were with the Boers, but still he felt loyalty to the British and this impelled him to assist on their side. He believed that only in the British Empire could India be relieved of foreign rule and stand on her own. He quickly offered the services of a corps that he himself had raised, but, true to the form they had displayed at the time, the Government told him that his services were not required. Even so, he managed to be present as a stretcher-bearer at Colenso and when sense prevailed the Government agreed that there was work for them to do, but stated that the Indians, 1100 strong, were not to be allowed within range of gunfire.

After Spion Kop, this changed too and General Buller informed Ghandi that the Government would be grateful if his men could serve as stretcher-bearers, typically adding the rider that that he could not force them. They undertook the humanitarian work willingly, often marching 20 to 25 miles per day carrying wounded back to the field dressing stations and hospitals. Private soldiers thought well of them and there appear to have been cordial relations between both parties. Buller mentioned them in his despatches and no doubt this assisted Ghandi and 36 others of his Indian Ambulance Corps to be awarded the War Medal.

One wonders what happened to the cordiality when peace set in.

In the case of Sergeant (as he then was) Frank E Talbot of 42nd Battery RFA, an Indian apothecary was recalled for the rest of his life. This man, named Amoor, came with the battery from India and was gratefully remembered for his ability to stop the men's dysentery with his herb concoctions.

Sergeant Talbot could serve as a type for the long-service soldiers who were the army's backbone. His grandson, Mr. John T Stanton of Leeds, had a paternal grandfather who was killed at Hill 60, and Mr. Talbot was his mother's father. The family has faithfully saved their memorabilia and from Frank Talbot's documents it is found that he joined up at the age of 12 or 13 in May 1889 when he was 4ft 11.½"in height. By March of '92 he had grown to 5ft 9". In the 90s he was mainly at Woolwich and Sheerness while regularly re-qualifying for further promotion. He was made corporal in April 1897 before the unit embarked for India at the end of that year. They were one of those hurriedly moved to South Africa as the situation deteriorated.

The endless pulse of garrison life continued and on 22 November one of Scott's long 12-pounders was moved from Gordon Hill to Cove Redoubt. A more newsworthy item, however, was the capture by the Boers of 228 oxen, worth £8000, that had strayed towards their lines. The Boer artillery played the role of cowherd and brought them home by firing just over and behind them.

Presumably, to the Boers, the beasts meant tractive power rather than meat, but the event was meat and drink to *The Ladysmith Lyre*. The second issue of this prestigious mouthpiece carried the item,

'Whisky is selling at 35/- a bottle. The Army Service Corps is waiting until the price is two pounds before disposing of the eleven thousand bottles in stock. They desire that the garrison should have the opportunity of contributing indirectly to the cost of the two hundred and thirty head of transport oxen presented to the Boers the other day.' [At Christmas 1899 the British newspapers advertised whisky at 10/- a gallon, or a superior brand at 3/- per quart!]

But the *Lyre's* report came a little later, and, for immediate variety, the next night, that of the 23rd/24th, an empty locomotive filled with explosive charges was set off up the Orange Free State line to ram a Boer train but, unfortunately it turned over on a curve.

The unreality of life as seen from underneath the arches of shellfire is demonstrated by the fact that despite all this absorption with self, the immured could watch events outside. Natives got in and out of Ladysmith with news, at great danger to themselves, because of course the Boers would not hesitate to shoot them if caught. Also, carrier pigeons were in regular use. Only now, on the 25th, after a month of falling morale, could they be cheered by news from beyond the pale. General Buller had arrived in Natal.

Little did they know that much more pain and grief were in store before he was to arrive in Ladysmith.

It was on the 27th, when things were beginning to deteriorate noticeably, that humour asserted itself, and the *Ladysmith Lyre* burst on the scene. It was priced at 6d. per copy, so it was not cheap, and its opening prospectus read,

'the *Ladysmith Lyre* is published to supply a long felt want. What you want in a besieged town, cut off from the world, is news which you can absolutely rely on as false. The rumours that pass from tongue to tongue may, for all you know, be occasionally true. Our news we guarantee to be false.'

The paper included;

'Latest Lyres.

From our own despondents

(by Wireless Telegraphy)

London November 5th'

'A shell from Long Tom burst in the War Office this afternoon. General Brackenbury, Director General of Ordnance, accepted its arrival with resignation. Several reputations were seriously damaged. Unfortunately the Ordnance Committee was not sitting. A splinter broke through into the Foreign Office and disturbed the siesta of the Prime Minister. [Lord Salisbury was serving as Prime Minister and Foreign Secretary.]'

Another such humorous paper, *The Ladysmith Bombshell,* did its work in keeping up public morale.

On November 7th full rations were reduced to: fresh meat (horse) 1.1/4 pounds, cooked horse meat 1/4 lb, three ounces mealie meal, one biscuit, tea or coffee 1/6th oz, sugar 1 oz, salt 1/4 oz, pepper 1/64th oz, mustard 1/20th oz, vinegar 1/10th oz, Chevril 1/3rd pint.

As November drew to a close, a night-sortie on the 30th silenced a Creusot on Middle Hill, 9 gunners being killed or wounded in the process. Against that, Ladysmith Town Hall was shelled and there were casualties. In spite of growing food shortages, *The Life of a Regiment* tells us that the Gordon Highlanders' officers managed to celebrate Saint Andrew's Day with 'Scotch Broth, salmon mayonnaise, haggis, saddle of mutton, turkey and ham, asparagus and fruit salad. The haggis was made by the master cook.'

December brought visible contact with the relief, if relief there was to be, when on the first day of the month heliograph contact was made with Weenen, 35 miles away. Harry Dick Cunyngham disclosed to his journal,

> 'We are quite safe here and the continual shelling is the only trouble we have - they calculate the Boers shot 5000 shells into Ladysmith last month and a shell burst in the Town Hall yesterday where some wounded were, killed one poor man, wounded six others. The Geneva Cross is flying over the building the same as it is at the convent and sanatorium. They do not appear to mind that.'

Meanwhile, General Buller was steadily preparing. He was now at Frere and Captain E. P. Jones *(HMS Forte)* joined his force with detachments from *HMS Forte, Terrible* and *Tartar* bringing two 4.7s and fourteen 12-pounders.

The *Ladysmith Lyre,* on December 5th, carried a story that illustrated the desire of the besieged to laugh at themselves and their enemies. We must remember that they had no idea if or when they would be relieved.

'The Relief of Ladysmith
Reprinted from the Times of December 5th, 2099.
A Wonderful Discovery

The eminent German archaeologist, Dr. Poompschiffer, has recently contributed to science the most interesting discovery of the century. It will be remembered that the learned professor started in the spring on a tour of exploration among the buried cities of Natal. When last heard of, in October, he had excavated the remains of Maritzburg and Estcourt, and was cutting his way through the dense primeval forests on the banks of the Tugela. By cable yesterday came intelligence of even more sensational finds. Briefly, Dr. Poompschiffer has re-discovered the forgotten town of Ladysmith. Crossing the Tugela, the intrepid explorer pushed northward. The dense bush restricted his progress to three miles a day. On the third day Poompschiffer noticed strange booming sounds frequently repeated; none of his party could guess what they were and curiosity ran high. On the sixth day the mystery was explained. The party came suddenly upon a group of what were at first taken for a species of extinct reptile, but which the profound learning of Poompschiffer enabled him to recognise as THE LAST SURVIVALS OF THE PREHISTORIC BOERS. Their appearance was almost terrifying. They were all extremely old. Their white beards had grown till they trailed beneath their feet, and it was the custom of the field-cornets to knee-halter each man at night with his own beard to prevent him running away. Their clothes had fallen to pieces with age, but a thick and impenetrable coating of dust and melinite [a French explosive of the day] saved their decency. Their occupation was as quaint as their appearance. They were firing obsolete machines, conjectured to be the cannon of the ancients, in the direction of a heap of cactus-grown ruins. That heap of ruins was the fabled fortress of Ladysmith.

Students of history will remember the Boer War of 1899, from which public attention was distracted by the Great War Office Strike. The learned will also remember at a later period, after the closing of that office, the controversy in our columns on the question whether Ladysmith existed or not, which the general voice of experts finally decided in the negative. It is now proved that so-called savants of that rude age were mistaken. Not only did Ladysmith exist, not only was it besieged, but up to the day before yesterday

The Siege of Ladysmith was still going on

The site of the town at first appeared uninhabited. But when Poompschiffer commenced excavating he came, to his amazement, upon signs of old workings at a depth of only a few feet below the surface. For an instant, he tells us, he thought some other antiquarian had been before him. Next moment some creature blundered along the tunnel into his very arms. It was secured and brought into the light. It was the last inhabitant of Ladysmith. It was apparently of the children born since the siege, and was about a hundred years old. From living in underground holes it was bent double and quite blind. It appeared to unable to speak, only repeating constantly, in a crooning voice, the syllables, "Weeskee, weeskee," which Poompschiffer was unable to translate. The professor was anxious to secure this unique specimen for the Kaiser William Museum of Antiquities at Berlin. But the moment it was removed from Ladysmith it began to pine away. Having never known any state of life but bombardment it was terrified by the absence of artillery fire. Time after time it attempted to escape to its native shells. Poompschiffer endeavoured to maintain life by artificial bombardment, letting off crackers in its ear and pelting it with large stones. But all was in vain, the extraordinary creature was not deceived, and in a few hours, with a last despairing wail of "Weeskee," it expired through sheer terror at the safety of its surroundings.'

Two days after the publication of this fable Major-General Sir Archibald Hunter, White's Chief of Staff, obtained a heartening result when he commanded a night attack on Gun Hill. Four hundred Natal Carbineers, 100 Imperial Light Horsemen and some Royal Engineers marched out from Devonshire Post at 10.15 pm. following the road between Long Hill and Gun Hill. By 2.00 am the assault party was ready to ascend the hill with Colonel Edwards, who was later wounded at Caesar's Camp, and Major Karri Davies and their ILH to the left of the Carbineers. The Boers had a keen memory of their grandfathers facing the Zulu assegais and they fled as the British cried out 'cold steel', pretending to fix bayonets before they rushed the crest. Quickly Long Tom was disabled along with its companion 4.7" howitzer, the breech-block a trophy, in spite of its 80 lb weight. It can now be seen in the Siege Museum. Two companies of Liverpools and a squadron of 19th Hussars captured Limit Hill, destroying the telephone line between Lombard's Kop and Joubert's laager at Modder Spruit. A force was sent up the road towards Elandslaagte but was driven back with 3 killed, 3 officers and 18 men wounded.

The destruction of Long Tom was received with delight, but he was not dead, only circumcised, and he and the damaged howitzer were taken to Pretoria for repair. He then re-appeared at Kimberley, much to that garrison's unhappiness.

The jaws of the siege clenched harder and the price of necessities was made further subject to the amended and exaggerated laws of supply and demand, with whisky at 21/- per bottle and butter at 5/- per lb. [In England it was 1/- a pound.]

HMS *Forte's* Signal Apparatus.

On the night of the 10th/11th General Howard mounted an attack on the 4.7" Howitzer on Surprise Hill which was only partially successful; 14 men dying with 50 wounded. While they were out on the veld, however, there was further encouraging proof of the possibility of life after the siege. As they sheltered, awaiting moonset, they watched reflected light flickering on clouds to the south. The inventive Captain Percy Scott had pulled off another coup by mounting a searchlight on a railway truck, which was driven towards Chieveley. The light was fronted with a venetian blind and when it was aimed at the clouds, the besiegers could read the Natal Field Force's Morse code. Interestingly, the forerunner of the electric signalling lamp had been born.

Sergeant-Major Walter Shaw again,

> 'One morning about the 10th of Dec. the Boers sent a shell into the officers mess of the Devonshire Regiment, killing two officers and wounding six others. Another shell was fired into the cavalry camp, which killed six men, wounded ten, and killed several horses. These instances are what are occurring daily, only of course not so severe, so they will give you a little idea of what we have to put up with.'

On 13th December, Lieutenant Colonel Dick Cunyngham returned to duty 'feeling very well, arm and fingers still stiff but getting stronger daily.' He was just in time to hand in his sword along with the other officers, and to be issued with a carbine.

December 16th is 'Dingaan's Day' when the Boers celebrate the defeat of the Zulu king of that name at Blood River in 1838. In 1899 as in other years they were on holiday but though the British could rest too, they still had their party of men ready to move at a moment's notice - 54 wagons, 16 men to a wagon. This arrangement was eventually discontinued as in one night parade when the Devonshire Regiment was on duty, their 'galloping mule-carts collided with the Terrible and the Powerful, the Ladysmith town filth carts, which were on their odorous rounds.' [Tommy Atkins' names for these vehicles were those of the Navy's latest cruisers, of course.]

The idea of making officers inconspicuous by their exchanging swords for carbines was carried a stage farther on the 18th when the Gordons returned their sporrans into store and sewed khaki aprons on to their kilts. It was fitting as in the Manchesters' account of the battle of Elandslaagte the note is made,

'Gordons' dark kilts afforded excellent targets and they suffered heavily in consequence.'

As Christmas approached much more quickly than General Buller did, White was sick in bed when the shell from 'Puffing Billy' struck 16, Poort Road, his HQ, to which reference was made earlier. A shell from the same gun landed in the camp of the Gloucesters on Junction Hill, killing six and wounding nine men.

16, Poort Road is an easy place to find, and though private property and much modernised, White, Hunter and Rawlinson would recognize it.

The writer was interested by a vast tree that grows in front of it, which had, apparently, grown since the war.

After the reverses of Black Week, there may have been some bitterness in the report made by Pearse of the *Daily News* on the 23rd, but with Spion Kop in mind, it was a prophetic quote too. A Boer was talking to a British officer about the prospects. 'We admit,' he said, 'the British soldiers are the bravest in the world, and your regimental officers the bravest, but - we rely on your generals.'

On Christmas Day there were almost 500 diseased patients in Intombi and in town food prices were still climbing. A Sports Meeting included an inter-services tug-of-war while Colonel Frank Rhodes and Major Karri Davies organized a party for 250 white children - all in a temperature of 103° in the shade. The Boers fired a shell marked with the flags of the South African republics, and 'With the compliments of the season.' It was filled with Christmas Pudding. Once the bun-fights were over, however, the only thing biting with any gusto would be the siege itself. The animal food was exhausted and the besieged were now reduced to horses and oxen - and there were only 181 rounds left for the 4.7s.

On Boxing Day, according to Louis Creswicke, 178 shells fell into the town before nine in the morning, not counting the fire of the Maxim Guns, and it was reported that a hundred or so Boer women could be seen watching the falls.

Supplies were running out at Intombi as well as in town, so that biscuits had to be crushed for the patients' food. Bandages were re-washed, household linen cut up for swabs. Added to this unpleasantness were the millions of flies, scorpions, tarantulas and centipedes. Some 560 men ended up in the graveyard, only about 40 of them due to wounds, the rest succumbing to disease.

The Boers let the New Year in with another joke. It was one quite funny enough to be capable of knocking down a house and killing the occupants, but it lacked a fuse, again wishing the recipients the compliments of the season. Dick Cunyngham wrote,

'A happy new year [sic] to you all. I hope you get news of us occasionally and you will know that I am alright and my arm gets stronger daily. I may get a year's blood money, £300, but the Board on wounded officers has not said yet...The siege has now lasted 9 weeks. If the Boers are driven back from here we shall not be able to advance for some time. Ammunition, clothing stores of all sorts will be required. The bridges at Colenso rebuilt, the railway mended, our transport renewed and many other things needed before we take the field again. At one time I thought we should get back to India in April - but the Cape Rebels and F/S joining has made it a tremendous and serious affair and if we are driven back [?] from their present position north of the Tugela that they will then fall back on the

Site of Intombi Camp, Umbulwana at rear. COURTESY OF STEVE A WATT

The Six Inch Gun

There is a famous hill looks down
Five miles away, on Ladysmith town,
With a long flat ridge that meets the sky
Almost a thousand feet on high
    And on the ridge there is mounted one
    Long-range terrible six inch gun.

And down in the street a bugle is blown
When, the cloud of smoke on the sky is thrown
For its sixty seconds before the roar
Reverberates o'er, and a second more
    Till the shell comes down with a whiz and stun
    From that long range terrible six inch gun.

And men and women walk up and down
The long hot streets of Ladysmith town
And the housewives work in the usual round
And the children play till the warning sound
    Then into their holes they scurry and run
    From the whistling shell of the six inch Gun

For the shells they weigh a hundred pounds
Bursting wherever they strike the ground
While the strong concussion shakes the air
And shatters the window panes everywhere
    And we may laugh, but there's little of fun
    In the bursting shell from a six inch gun.

Oh! 'twas whistle and jest with the cartineers gay
As they cleaned their steeds at break of day.
But like a thunderclap there fell
In the midst of the horses and men a shell
    And the sight we saw was a fearful one
    After that shell from the Six inch gun

Though the foe may beset us on every side
We'll find some cheer in this Christmas tide
We will laugh and be gay, but a tear will be shed
And a thought be given to the gallant dead
    Cut off in the midst of their life and fun
    By the long-range terrible six inch gun.

A contemporary piece of poetry celebrating the shelling.

Biggarsberg, then to the Drakensberg after that Pretoria...'

Dick Cunyngham had seen the truth of Britain's difficulties, of course, but an event was about to take place that would, sadly, render him incapable of more than that foresight.

Ladysmith has, quite understandably, made a business of the siege and among all the activity of a modern city it is evident everywhere. The focus is at the handsome Town Hall and the Siege Museum next door. Here are artefacts, maps, photographs and other presentations, and outside are the old howitzers, Castor and Pollux, with the replica of Long Tom. Scattered about town are numerous marked sites and memorials, some, sadly, vandalised or as in the case of the Leicesters plaque on Observation Hill, weathered, and the town offers a very useful guide called Historic Ladysmith - Focus on Siegetown.

The starting place has to be the Siege Museum

1 *'The Royal Irish Fusiliers 1793 - 1950'* by Marcus Cunliffe.

Dragoon Guards Monument, vandalized in 1997.

Chapter Five

PLATRAND 5/6 JAN 1900

A Boer Krygsraad early in January decided to capture the Platrand, and the attempt turned out to be the crucial battle of the siege. Each of the Boer armies would provide 2000 men, supplemented by 600 of Louis Botha's burghers for an attack on the Platrand. The plan was for Wagon Hill to be the responsibility of the Free Staters, with Winburgers attending to the main southern face and some four hundred of the Harrismith, Heilbron, and Kroonstad men climbing Wagon Point and the western end of Wagon Hill. C. J. de Villiers, a veteran of Majuba, led them. The Transvaalers would deal with Caesar's Camp. See map page 82 Six hundred men of the Vryheid and German commandos would climb the southern slope and, at the same time, men from Heidelberg, Wakkerstroom, Standerton, Krugersdorp and Utrecht would assault the eastern end - 900 in all, under the direction of Schalk Burger. Botha's men were to form the reserve. A diversion against Observation Hill was planned, with aggressive activity round the whole perimeter.

On the British side there were two squadrons of ILH on Wagon Hill (38men), and Wagon Point (41 men), and a body of 2/King's Royal Rifle Corps under Major H. Gore-Browne. Caesar's Camp was manned by men of the 1/Manchesters in small enclosures or forts, directed

Cemetery on Caeser's Camp.

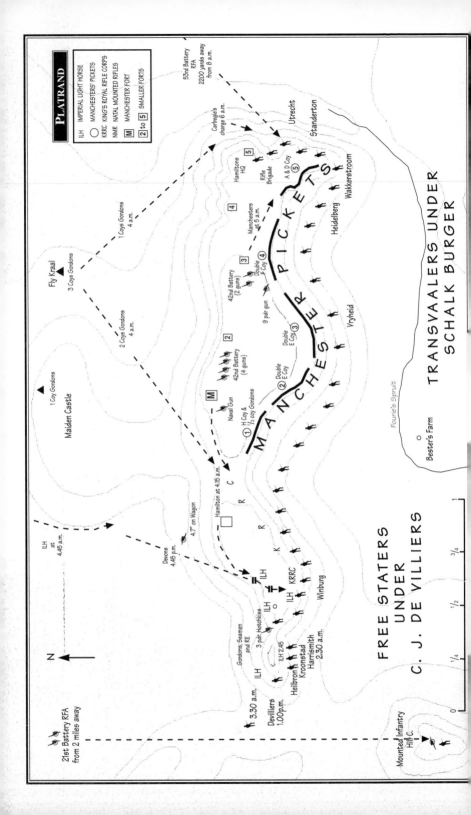

Bester's Valley from Ceasar's Camp.

from the larger Manchester Fort near the Wagon Hill end of Caesar's - they had been on the hill since the October. When they arrived it was impossible to get wagons within 1¹/₂ miles of the camp, so everything was carried up with pack mule and fatigues. The *Diary of Siege of Ladysmith* in the archive of the Manchester Regiment in Stalybridge Public Library records the development of the defences on the hill from then onward, along with the occasional bursts of violent activity. An interesting entry on the 15th December shows that 'Captain Menzies and Lieutenant Roe with 30 men proceeded to Bester's Farm to cover 75 coolies sent to dig potatoes etc. - they could not find any.' A note in Ladysmith Siege Museum records that a sortie on December 23rd was more successful, collecting 43 geese and 6 pigs. Bester's Farm was Boer territory under the south face of the Platrand - not a good place to be a fortnight later, on January 6th.

Manchester Fort, Caesar's Camp.

On the 7th November the 42nd Battery RFA had taken position on the left of Manchester Fort, and on the 8th two more guns came up and took position near Fort 3. Sailors brought a 12-pounder and a 9-pounder, and a detachment of the Natal Naval Volunteers was equipped with a Hotchkiss machine-gun. At the very end of the Platrand was a smaller, fifth fort. The whole plateau was, and is, covered with brush and the inevitable red rocks; plenty of them of such size as to give rifleman good cover. To make things more difficult, in the dark the attackers would look very like the ILH whose soft hats had the brim pinned up on the left-hand side.

The Boers moved off at midnight on the 5th/6th January at the same time as a party of men was working on gun emplacements on Wagon Hill: thirty-three sappers worked under Lieutenant R. J. T. Digby Jones RE, with Gunner Sims and 13 bluejackets from HMS *Powerful*. They were re-positioning the Junction Hill gun, Lady Anne, which was still in a wagon at the foot of the hill.

60 Gordon Highlanders from Fly Kraal joined the forty-odd sailors and engineers around 1.00am to unload. The ILH picket on the southern slope of Wagon Point heard the sounds of climbing men and a volley fired down the hill precipitated a response from the attackers. In minutes, a close-quarter struggle was in progress, briefly lit up when Captain Matthias' (ILH) fired the Hotchkiss down the hill. The sailors and engineers of the working party stopped work and lined up in the emplacement, but the Gordons had to retrieve their arms were from stacks, and, as they returned to the line, they blundered into the attackers. Some were temporarily made prisoners.

Today there is a shopping complex on the old cricket field, the 'Oval', wherein the elaborate little cricket pavilion familiar to the troops and home to the nurses is now hidden but recognizable. The shopper who turns right into Murchison Street's bustle still passes the Town Hall to the right before the Royal and Crown Hotels on the left, and he or she is still conscious of the hills above. Convent Hill is nearby and above to the right behind the Oval; Umbulwana is glimpsed down the side-roads to the left, further away but massive; and in front is the continuous wall of the Platrand. This Boer name seems a better, unified title than those the British used, but, for the troops, Caesar's Camp harked back to the base at home in Aldershot.

Below it, at the bottom of town, where the T-junction is enforced by the course of the Klip River, the scene, and the public appreciation of the scene, is Wimpy. It is a navigating mark, like a British city pub; here 'Carry on down to Wimpy,' was said to the author, and the useful historical walking guide produced by the Ladysmith Publicity Association says laconically, 'Proceed to Wimpy.' Raise the eyes above the fast food shop though and the romantically named Settlers Park is seen. To the right, the road out of town crosses Wagon Bridge, and across the river, admittedly over the top of industrial property, is the ridge that was the bone of contention that night.

It is some 3000 metres from Ladysmith town centre, and running roughly west to east, with a higher point at each end and a steep face on its far, south side dropping into Bester's Valley.

Captain Mathias ordered his men back to the crest and, outlined against the sky, they made good targets for the enemy before they could gain the shelter of their hilltop fort. At one point he was among the Boers but escaped detection and got back to his command. Meanwhile at the extreme end of Wagon Point, the men guarding the 4.7″ gun repelled a party of attackers.

Ian Hamilton, in command, was awakened from his sleep at the rear of the eastern end of Caesar's Camp and he immediately sent to Fly Kraal for three companies of Gordon Highlanders. Captain the Hon. R. F. Carnegie took one company to reinforce the Manchesters at Caesar's Camp, and two went to Wagon Hill. Hamilton then set off for Manchester Fort where Colonel Curran, commanding the Manchesters, had already ensured that the pickets standing down remained at their posts with their replacements at 3.30 am.

Hamilton left Curran in charge of Caesar's Camp and continued to the KRRC position on Wagon Hill. Here Major Gore-Browne briefed him and, in turn, he telephoned Sir George White. The General directed the remaining three squadrons of the ILH to Wagon Hill, and the rest of the Gordons were moved up from their camp to Fly Kraal. It was now that Dick Cunyngham, VC, was killed. We saw the last entry in his diary in the previous chapter. It was written on New Year's Day and included some perceptive opinions on the British situation before the entry petered out. The diary concludes with someone else's remark,

Colonel Ian Hamilton.

'(Left unfinished) "Caesar's Camp 6th January was the end for this brave life."'

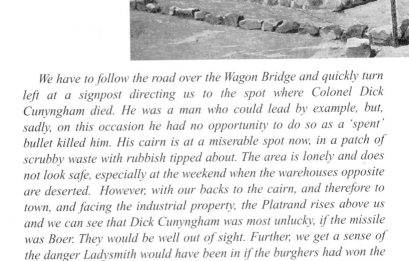

Dick Cunyngham's Cairn now, and then.

We have to follow the road over the Wagon Bridge and quickly turn left at a signpost directing us to the spot where Colonel Dick Cunyngham died. He was a man who could lead by example, but, sadly, on this occasion he had no opportunity to do so as a 'spent' bullet killed him. His cairn is at a miserable spot now, in a patch of scrubby waste with rubbish tipped about. The area is lonely and does not look safe, especially at the weekend when the warehouses opposite are deserted. However, with our backs to the cairn, and therefore to town, and facing the industrial property, the Platrand rises above us and we can see that Dick Cunyngham was most unlucky, if the missile was Boer. They would be well out of sight. Further, we get a sense of the danger Ladysmith would have been in if the burghers had won the battle that night. The town would have been untenable.

By 4.15 am, the Manchesters had stayed the assault up the south face of Caesar's Camp, but at the far eastern end, the enemy emerged on the top near the extreme picket and turned west, attempting to take the Manchesters end on, but found A and D companies defending fiercely. The whole hillside was full of the enemy at daybreak and so there was a confused criss-cross of rifle-fire. The attackers could never move forward without killing those in the next sangar, but they made progress until Colonel Curran himself strengthened No. 3 fort. According to the Manchester Regiment's *Diary of the Siege of Ladysmith* at Stalybridge Public Library,

> 'Nearly all our men were shot in the head and arms while firing, and lay dead in their sangars, many were shot from behind and hanging over their sangars facing down the hill to their front.'

Meanwhile Captain the Hon. R F Carnegie, in command of G Company, Gordon Highlanders, strengthened the sangars at the north-eastern corner of the hill. Men of the Rifle Brigade joined the stretched garrison and the mixed party sustained a fearful battering from the invaders. Rifle fire elevated Captain John Gough to senior British Officer, but he had no one directing him and the numbers of the enemy were not clear.

Sergeant Talbot of the 42nd Battery said that at one point the Boers were only some 70 yards from his position in the gun emplacement. The gunners were using case shot, which burst quickly after leaving the gun's muzzle and sprayed an area up to 200 yards away.

Lieutenant Hunt-Grubbe, 1/Manchesters, went forward, unarmed, to the pickets and was taken prisoner. Carnegie saw two Boers on the crest and he shot one, thus announcing himself to the other and attracting a volley of fire. Now, at 6.00 am, he was saved by a sudden succession of shrapnel shells that burst over the attackers.

The 53rd Battery had been ordered up and Major Abdy brought it

Caesar's Camp defences, foreground.

into battle from some bushes near Fly Kraal, three miles or so down the road towards Intombi. In full view was the slope of Caesar's Camp covered with many Boers. Attacking them with shrapnel allowed Carnegie to move forward. The 53rd adjusted its fire and the Gordons drove the last few attackers from the crest with the bayonet. Colour-Sergeant Pryce killed a Boer before being mortally wounded himself and Carnegie shot four dead before he received wounds in arm and neck. But the Boers were now sheltered from the artillery and though Carnegie made little further progress, the crest was in British hands.

All morning the Creusot and a 15-pounder on Umbulwana had been shelling Caesar's Camp, when, it is believed, Mrs Joubert spotted Abdy's battery. However, the 155mm gun was hampered in turn by the attentions of the 4.7" at Cove Redoubt so that the Boers had difficulty in finding 53rd battery, they themselves being under fire. In fact, Captain H. Lambton's report to Sir George White stated that the gun at Cove Redoubt fired 28 rounds at Puffing Billy, 8500 yards away, and Abdy fired some 138 rounds during the action in spite of taking punishment. A Sergeant Boseley lost his left arm and leg to a shell.

A note in General White's diary on 22nd February appeared to refer to him when it said,

> '...sitting on the trail of the gun when a shell took one leg and one arm off. When he was struck down he called out to the men, "Here, roll me out of the way and go on with the work!"'

White said that in a fortnight he was out driving.

The 12-pounder at Gordon Hill was also shelling Umbulwana, while the one at Leicester Post engaged the enemy 12-pounder on Rifleman's Ridge and their 4.5" on Surprise Hill. The 12-pounder on Caesar's Camp engaged the enemy on Middle Hill.

The Manchesters and ILH, augmented by the KRRC and the Gordons, were now reinforced by the 5/Lancers and one hundred 19/Hussars with some Liverpool MI at the Caesar's Camp end of the Platrand, and the 18/Hussars on Wagon Hill.

Colonel Curran and the Manchesters, unaware of the Rifle Brigade behind them, were still under fire and Colonel Metcalfe sent two companies across open ground towards the rear of picket No. 5. Suddenly a massive volley met them. All the officers were wounded and the men were left without direction, in the open, and under fire, all day. *The Times History* says that Caesar's Camp was now really overcrowded, but Privates Pitts and Scott of the 1/Manchesters would not have agreed. We shall come to these two later.

On Wagon Hill things were even worse and Major Miller-Walnutt brought up more Gordon Highlanders as well as the rest of the ILH to face 250 Free Staters. The two sides were sometimes almost feet apart with, again, the Boers' new rifles making the difference. The soldiers could not see the smoke, nor could they fire as fast as the enemy, and what is more their leaders did not know what to do about it. Three small counter-attacks were initiated with men being killed. When Hamilton arrived on Wagon Hill there was a dangerous and confused situation. The 250 farmers, outnumbered as they were, controlled the centre of the crest and had support to the left and right, while the slope below them was filled with their comrades. Facing them was Captain Mathias and his few ILH hanging on like grim death. To their left were the KRRC scattered about in the straggle of rocks, or in the sangars. On the right, at the far end of Wagon Point and in the gun pits was the group of engineers, sailors, and Gordons fighting the Boers at the foot of the hill. Apparently the actual crest of Wagon Point was empty apart from a wagon with its oxen feeding quietly, in spite of the death and destruction around them. During the morning, all the Light Horse but five were wounded or killed, although they were responding to their attackers with equal effect.

Almost two miles away, 21st Battery RFA was positioned between Range Post and Sign Post Ridge, and began to fire at about 6.30 am. For the next hour it shelled Mounted Infantry Hill cutting down the fire of the Boer artillery and, as it turned out, stopping the introduction of a pom pom.

Drive back from Dick Cunyngham's cairn to the main road and turn left. Soon, heading towards Harrismith or Pietermaritzburg, suburbia comes to an abrupt stop on the right, and look for the sign for Platrand and Ladysmith Aerodrome just before the crest. Here, turn left, leaving the Ladysmith Motel and the airfield to the right.

Drive up on the Platrand where there will be found a dirt road overlooking Ladysmith on the left. Surprisingly, at the saddle between Caesar's Camp and Wagon Hill there is a gate. It has been seen to be propped open, but with the ominous warning that it is locked at 5.00 pm. Clearly it would not do to be locked in and it may be a good idea for the visitor to avoid the end of the day. Near here is a military cemetery beside the track.

As the rest of the ILH arrived, they were pushed up towards what was now the front line, and on to Wagon Point. Lord Ava, a messenger for Colonel Hamilton, fell dying and was brought to temporary safety by Colonel Frank Rhodes. Many other officers were killed or wounded

115

as they repeatedly tried to mount assaults on the Free Staters. New arrivals were quickly drafted in. So a kind of stalemate developed, with both sides lying out in the blazing sun, unable to move forward. C. J. De Villiers knew that his people were relatively safe where they were, but that to move forward would be murderous.

Lord Ava.

By late morning, the action having quietened down, Hamilton decided that as a respite from the great heat and because of their hunger some of the men could go down the hill to the rear for lunch. At 1.00 pm when Lieutenant Digby-Jones, Major Miller-Wallnutt, Gunner Sims and Hamilton were at the 4.7″ gun emplacement on Wagon Point, it was as if the lunch-break had ended. The Boers led by Field-Cornets Japie de Villiers and De Jager again surged over the crest, reaching the parapet of the gun-platform as they drove the British back. The senior officers were thus personally involved, and their men were not only eating, but some, we are told, were asleep.

Those in the emplacement fell back in shock, and began to flee but the officers, Gunner Sims and others managed to assert control and the Boers melted in the face of repeated volleys from the ILH in their sangar nearby. Just three attackers, De Villiers, De Jager, and Wessels

Caesar's Camp defences, foreground.

bravely hung on and raced with the British for the actual gun pits.

Hamilton, who must have thought it was Majuba all over again, was shooting at the Boers, Trooper Albrecht was firing from outside the pit, Digby Jones and Corporal Hockaday RE were also firing. Miller-Wallnutt fell dead, followed by Herman Albrecht, a lad from Aliwal, North Cape. He was 24 years of age. Digby Jones and Lieutenant Dennis RE., Japie De Villiers, De Jager and Wessels fell dead in turn. Sims lined his twelve men in extended order and charged with the bayonet, other British troops completing the repulse. The moment was saved and the enemy driven off, but at a high price.

Major Miller-Wallnutt, D.S.O.

In the Siege Museum an interesting diorama shows the moment. At the rear is the main emplacement, below it and nearer to us, on the right front, is another stretch of rough wall offering protection to the gun-pit. At its left-hand end is a lean-to, open side to us, of course, and another, centre-rear stage, to the left of and beside the actual pit. On the extreme left is a shelter with sandbagged walls and, near it, a bell-tent.

On one knee in the left foreground is Gunner Sims, aiming diagonally across the scene; to his right and nearest to us is the body of Lieutenant Digby Jones, newly killed. At the far edge of the gun-pit are De Jager, Japie De Villiers and Wessels, already dead or about to die bravely. With his back to us and just across the gun-pit from them is Hamilton, and, at his left elbow, the dying Miller-Wallnutt. It all catches the flavour and drama of the close confrontation.

Gunner Sims.

Losses among officers were particularly high. Apart from Lord Ava, there were Majors Doveton, Mackworth and Bowen, Lieutenants Pakeman, Raikes, and Tod killed, and Colonel Edwards, Karri Davies, and others wounded.

It appears that many of the enemy just never took part in the attack or fired from a distance away, thereby threatening their own men. The situation was now quite similar to that on Spion Kop a fortnight later. All day long, the opponents faced one another in

117

Lieutenant Digby-Jones.

blinding sunshine; often lying nearer to the enemy than a fast bowler is to the batsman at the start of his run-up, each hiding behind his rock and firing at the object of his whole attention, the thing that made the least movement.

The afternoon wore on and clouds began to fill the sky. As the rain began to fall in typically violent South African manner, the rifle fire again broke out with greater intensity. Boers feared a strong British attempt to drive them off, and they fired wildly into the rain. The British meanwhile were themselves confused, but at the eastern end of Caesar's the defenders appear to have grasped the situation more quickly, and the Manchesters' Mounted Infantry began to drive the Boers back down the southern slopes. The rain was easing off by 5.30 pm when the Gordons and KRRC hurried forward to join the Manchesters. The spirit of the Boers on Caesar's Camp was broken and they scrambled down the southern and south-eastern slopes into Fourie's Spruit, which was now in flood. Some were drowned, according to the *Times History*, and the rifle-fire and shrapnel from the 42nd Battery inflicted further casualties. Any attempt at stiffening them again was of no avail, and not even the appearance, at this point, of Botha himself could rectify the matter. It seemed that the Boers had shot their bolt.

At the orders of General White three companies of the 1/Devonshire Regiment, (nicknamed the "Bloody Eleventh" when known as the 11th Foot) had been brought up about five o'clock to drive the attackers off before nightfall. In his diary, Lieutenant Colonel C.W. Park wrote that his men were quickly in position and he was instructed by Colonel Hamilton to charge the party of Boers holding a rocky eminence at the end of Wagon Hill where the small nek leads to Wagon Point. It meant a race with fixed bayonets across bare ground. *The Times* of Tuesday, January 9th 1900 carried a copy of Buller's telegram sent from Frere to the War Office. It began,

> 'Following message just received from General White 2 pm yesterday...Some of our entrenchments on Wagon Hill were three times taken by the enemy and retaken by us. The attack continued until 7.30 pm. One point in our position was occupied by the enemy the whole of the day, but at dusk, in a very heavy rainstorm, they were turned out of the position at the point of the bayonet in the most gallant manner by the Devon Regiment led by Colonel Park.'

Hamilton and Park had made their way to the jumble of rocks held by

The charge of the Devons on Wagon Hill.

the IHL and others, and while they were sprayed by Mauser fire, Park was shown what was required.

The men formed up, and in gathering darkness while the lightning flashed and the rain fell, they prepared to make their charge. Lack of room meant that the approach had to be in column with F Company under Lieutenant Field charging straight across the open flat. E Company, commanded by Captain Lafone, had to wheel half right and thus prolong the line, while D Company under Lieutenant Masterson supported the centre of the charge. Bayonets were fixed and Colonel Park instructed the bugler to sound the advance. Park stood up and the men, breaking into wild cheering, charged into a blast of flame. Boers stood up too, as they did at Talana and other battles, firing as fast as they could. Again their five-round clip paid off, and the advancing soldiers were under at hail of bullets in the last of the light. They raced across the ground that had been contested in the sunshine all day with men falling. The line swerved to the right on Park's instruction, the men still cheering as they clambered into the group of rocks which had hidden the Boers all the afternoon. To their left, a company of Manchesters joined them and to their right was a mixed body of Light Horse and cavalry that extended the line. During the charge Lieutenant Hill, 5/Lancers, and Lieutenant Walker of the Somerset Light Infantry (attached), were killed and Captain Menzies wounded. In the rocks, Captain Lafone and Lieutenant Field were also killed, while Lieutenant Masterson earned himself a Victoria Cross by his bravery in going back for support.

As Commanding Officer of the 1/Devons, Lieutenant Colonel Park had taken command from Colonel Yule, who then commanded the retreat of the Dundee garrison. Park's diary reveals him as a gentle type of man in the privacy of his own thoughts and when Hamilton explained the task before him and asked him, straight out, if he could do it, his response was, 'We will try'. The two men were engulfed by rifle-fire and Park is like other commentators in hearing the rattle of Mauser fire as the crackle of dry burning twigs around them as they hurried along. As the violent storm developed and passed the Devons charged into the face of the Mausers on the ridge. They weathered both storms before taking the crest, only to find that the Boers had taken a new position further on.

Park wrote,

'We were still exposed to a heavy crossfire from both flanks, from which we suffered severely. Just then Lafone remarked that he wished someone would tell the Imperial Light Horse fellows, who were holding a little ridge behind us, to fire at the Boers on our left front, and, without a word, Masterson jumped up and ran back across the open through a hail of bullets to give the Imperial Light Horse the message, and though he was badly hit by at least three bullets in both thighs, he managed to reach them and give them the message, before he collapsed. It was a splendidly brave thing to do, and I have strongly recommended him for the VC. Very soon I was watching Lafone, who had got a rifle and was sniping

Lieutenant Colonel C. W. Park. at the Boers, when I suddenly saw a little hole come in his head just above his right ear, and he just sank down as he sat. I crawled over and found him quite dead, poor fellow, and a little further on I found poor Field, also lying dead. Walker (of the Somersets) had been shot dead during the charge, and about fifty-two men were either killed or wounded, and I was the only officer left.'

In the dark the Boers' made their escape, General De Villiers being the last to go.

The truce next morning preceded the petering out of the action and it was revealed that seventeen officers and 158 men were dead, with 28 officers and 221 men wounded. The Imperial Light Horse was

The Devons charged from the camera position towards the location of the car.

particularly hard hit with 8 officers out of 10 on Wagon Hill wounded.

Queen Victoria wrote to General White,

> 'Warmly congratulate you and all your command on your brilliant success. Greatly admire conduct of Devonshire Regiment.'

The County showed its admiration by presenting the two battalions of the Regiment with four silver side drums each commemorating their part in the Defence (1st Battalion) and Relief (2nd Battalion) of Ladysmith.

From where the gate is, turn off to the right onto Wagon Hill and the red-brown track winds through the long grass and scrub before coming to an open area bounded by bushes. In front, beyond the exposed section, is a rocky rise and beyond that the shallower nek leading to Wagon Point. To call the exposed area a green is to dignify it, but it is as bare as a village green, and as intimate; far smaller than a cricket field. Park, Lafone and the others must have been brave indeed.

Here Masterson won his VC, and on the Devonshire Monument by the rocks Lafone, Field and Walker have got their memorial with nineteen other ranks. "Semper Fidelis," it says.

Remembered here is Lord Ava, Colonel Hamilton's galloper, of whom it was said,

> 'He was the best type of Englishman - Irish-English - excellently made, delighting in his strength and all kinds of sport, his eye full of light, his voice singularly beautiful and attractive. His courage was extraordinary and did not come of ignorance.'

Devonshire's Monument on Wagon Hill.

121

ILH Monument, Wagon Hill.

He is buried in Ladysmith cemetery. Others remembered with or near him are the Imperial Light Horse, the Royal Engineers (including Lieutenant Digby-Jones), De Villiers, and, interestingly, Pastor J. D. Kestell, who stayed throughout the day comforting Boer and Briton alike as they lay wounded. Later, his son died in Ladysmith while a prisoner of war. It was the British who preserved the Pastor's memory with a memorial.

Returning to the gate, we continue forward onto Caesar's Camp and though the terrain is similar, we are on a much broader plateau stretching away towards a distant compound at the end with what looks like a wireless station in it. There is today plenty of cover for infantry, at least in September/October after the southern winter. The need for company was highlighted by the fact that when the writer saw the path to the Manchester Fort, certain young local men were observed, head and shoulders only. At first, they seemed to be doing nothing meaningful, and it

J.D. Kestell's marker on Wagon Hill.

IT WAS HERE THAT DURING THE BATTLE ON 6TH
JANUARY, 1900, THE REVEREND JOHN DANIEL
KESTELL, MINISTER OF THE HARRISMITH COMMANDO,
IN GREAT DANGER AND UNDER HEAVY FIRE
BROUGHT SUCCOUR TO WOUNDED FRIEND AND FOE
ALIKE

A GRIEVOUSLY WOUNDED BRITISH SERGEANT SAID TO
HIM
"YOU ARE PREACHING A GOOD SERMON TO-DAY."

OP HIERDIE PLEK GEDURENDE DIE VELDSLAG OP 6
JANUARIE 1900 HET DS. JOHN DANIEL KESTELL,
VELDPREDIKER VAN DIE KOMMANDO VAN HARRISMITH,
MET LEWENSGEVAAR EN ONDER HEWIGE GEWEERVUUR
HULP VERLEEN AAN GEWONDE VRIEND EN VYAND
SONDER ONDERSKEID

DIS TOE DAT 'N SWAARGEWONDE BRITSE SERSANT
AAN DS. KESTELL GESÊ HET:
"HIERDIE DAAD VAN U IS 'N TREFFENDE PREEK".

ERECTED AT THE WISH OF BRITISH SOLDIERS

was worrying that youngsters were hanging about there. Only as the path unwound, was it clear that they were council workers tidying up the site after the winter and they were as cautious about the old white man approaching as he was about them!

No harm done, but it should be remembered at all times that there is safety in numbers.

Scattered about in the roughs is the Monument to the 18/Hussars, marking their position and that of the 1/Manchesters and common graves for their comrades. Nearby, on the town side, is Manchester Fort, the substantial dry-stone walled HQ of that regiment.

Of the decorations earned in the action, Albrecht, Digby-Jones and Masterson won VCs, and there were two for privates in the 1/Manchester Regiment. An unnamed reporter of the Manchester Guardian interviewed them and the piece, dated April 17th, appeared in that paper on 18th May 1900, by which time Scott was a Corporal.

Private Pitts, from Blackburn and aged 23, said that he began firing at 3.30 am and his picket was reliant on its own resources till the afternoon when the Rifle Brigade came up. He appeared to have been too busy to know that they had been firing from his rear for some time earlier. The range was amazingly short. The Boers were, he said, within sixteen yards of him, and it was death to appear over the rock.

His companion, Private Robert Scott, was a 26 year-old from Haslingden, also of D Company. Quite soon he began to believe that all was lost. The left of the line was gone, the Boers advanced as though nothing could stop them, and he fully expected a rush that would result either in his death or capture. After a while, however, he discovered that the Boer leaders were in difficulties as great as those of our own people were - they could not get their men to come up. He could hear the commandant - a brave man, whoever he was - urging and calling on his men to come forward and sweep away the little handful of Manchesters who still clung to the crest; but exhortations were to little purpose and the rank and file of the Boers hung back. Lieutenant Hunt Grubbe, who was held as a prisoner by the Boers for most of the day, confirmed this as he saw the commandant run back from the firing line time and again to urge and implore the supports to advance.[1]

Scott ran out of ammunition but he and Pitt helped themselves to that of two of their dead comrades in the sangar with them. Scott got up to look for reinforcements and was at once struck in the face by several splinters; 'so I had to duck down again'. Just before this Pitts and Murphy, one of those from whom they subsequently got ammunition, had also stood up for a minute and Murphy had been instantly killed.

Scott warned Pitts to be careful but, after a minute or two, Pitts moved again, ever so little. This was enough for the watchful Boer who had slain Murphy; he showed himself just for a moment and Scott shot him dead, sending him rolling down the hill.

So, for holding a sangar for fifteen hours without food and water, all the time under extremely heavy fire from Boers in sangars immediately to their left rear, the two were eventually cited in the *London Gazette* on the 26th of July 1901 as recipients of the Victoria Cross.

In Stalybridge Public Library is a copy of Captain Vizard's report,

Private James Pitts VC, 1/Manchesters.

'These men occupied a sangar on the left of which all our men had been shot down, and their positions occupied by the Boers. Consequently they were all the time under an extremely heavy fire. The case had been referred to by Sir G. White, and in the press on different occasions.

The valour displayed by these men was remarkable, they held this post for 15 hours without food or water - as this picquet [sic] was about to be relieved when the attack opened. Private Scott was wounded and there were many killed and wounded on all sides of them.'

Hamilton, at the unveiling of the Manchester Regiment Memorial in that city, (see page 64) said,

Private Robert Scott VC, 1/Manchesters.

'[in] Ladysmith the Manchesters had to stand the slow and sapping struggle against starvation at Caesar's Camp, where want, like an armed man, rushed on your lads and struck them down as they were staggering forward to meet the bullets of the foe. The Manchesters covered themselves with glory there. They never did better. They fought against starvation from 2.30 on the morning of the 6th January till 5.30 in the afternoon. Those starving, ragged lads kept back the Boers from the vitals of the town.'

The Burgher Memorial dominates the whole of Caesar's Camp. It is a group of huge stylised hands built on a platform and reaching up to the sky. Below the group are the remains of 310 Boers who were re-buried here along with a Roll of Honour. Sadly that has been stolen; another manifestation of the vandalism that has been experienced in Ladysmith, at Colenso and elsewhere.

Caesar's Camp. Platrand
Boer Memorial.

The British won the day with the usual doggedness and bravery by officer and man alike, but it is also true that the Boers failed anyway. To begin with, there was no De Wet or De La Rey, of course, and no Botha until late in the day, but the senior officers in the area, Prinsloo, Schalk Burger[2], and the Commandant General, Joubert himself, were not up to it. The commanders on the hill were too closely involved in the fighting to have an overview and most of the men committed to the assault by the *krygsraad* never attempted to join in. Even the artillery were unprepared, with the 155mm Creusot on Telegraph Hill having only three shells available at the start of the battle.

As it turned out, the action on Caesar's Camp and Wagon Hill was the last serious one of the siege. It resulted in the death of 14 British Officers and 135 NCOs and men. Three officers died of wounds and so did 23 other ranks. The wounded numbered 28 officers and 221 NCOs and men.

1 Hunt Grubbe's short captivity was useful in that he saw why it was so difficult to verify the Boer losses. At one point he counted 27 dead, but noted that the enemy always sent their dead and wounded to the rear, and because of this it was impossible to prove or disprove their reported casualties.
2 Schalk Burger: 'a most inferior soldier', Lieutenant-Colonel C J Blomfield DSO, commanding 2/Lancashire Fusiliers on Spion Kop.

BURGERGEDENKTEKEN
DIE BEELDE STEL HANDE VOOR EN DUI IN DIE RIGTING VAN DIE SLAGVELDE WAAR DIE BURGERS GESTERF HET
DIE HANDE VERBEELD STOERHEID ONVERSKROKKENHEID VREESLOOSHEID ASOOK ANGS LYDING SMART
DIE BESKERMENDE HANDE OMSLUIT DIE BOGIES EN REIK MET GELOOF NA BO
791 BURGERS HET GEDURENDE DIE ANGLO-BOEREOORLOG VAN 1899-1902 IN DIE STRYD IN NATAL DIE HOOGSTE OFFER GEBRING
IN DIE GRAFKELDER RUS DIE BEENDERE VAN 310 VAN DIE OORLEDENES DIE ANDER (A GEMERK) IS ELDERS BEGRAWE
2 DOGTERTJIES IS ONDERSKEIDELIK IN DIE BOEREKRYGSGEVANGENEKAMP EN IN DIE KONSENTRASIEKAMP OP LADYSMITH OORLEDE

DEUR HIERDIE HANDE HET 'N GROTER HAND GESTORTE BLOED SO MILDELIK GESPROEI DAT VINGERTOPPE OOR DIE HEUWELLAND NA AKKERS WYS WAARUIT DIE VRYHEID GROEI
ERNST VAN HEERDEN

BURGHER MONUMENT
THE PILLARS PORTRAY HANDS AND POINT IN THE DIRECTION OF THE BATTLEFIELDS WHERE THE BURGHERS LOST THEIR LIVES
THESE HANDS REPRESENT STURDINESS INTREPIDNESS FEARLESSNESS AS WELL AS ANGUISH SUFFERING SORROW
THE PROTECTIVE HANDS SURROUND THE REMAINS OF THE DEAD AND REACH UPWARDS IN FAITH
791 BURGHERS MADE THE SUPREME SACRIFICE IN THE CAMPAIGN IN NATAL DURING THE ANGLO-BOER WAR OF 1899-1902
THE REMAINS OF 310 BURGHERS REST IN THE CRYPT THE REST (MARKED WITH AN *) ARE BURIED ELSEWHERE
TWO SMALL GIRLS DIED ONE IN THE BOER PRISONER OF WAR CAMP AND ONE IN THE CONCENTRATION CAMP AT LADYSMITH

Caesar's Camp. Platrand Boer Memorial showing upraised hands.

Chapter Six

AFTER PLATRAND, AND AFTERWARD STILL...

Two curious notes in separate archives highlight once more the bitter humour that soldiers are invariably capable of seeing in any grim situation.

One of the non-conformist hymns of the day, probably better known to any of the chapel-going rank and file than to their officers, ran, 'Hold the fort for I am coming, Jesus signals still.' In the archives of the Lancashire Regiment at Preston Barracks, there is the booklet, *'From Preston to Ladysmith,'* by T. Neligan. On page 16 we read,

> 'When at Frere, members of the South Lancashire Regiment
> found a Natal paper, a cutting from which ran:
> "Hold the fort for I am coming,"
> flashed the helio;
> Quick as lights, returns the answer,
> "Aren't you coming slow."'

Evidently this ditty tickled the soldiers' fancies in spite of the bad situation, and was even submitted to a variety of Chinese Whispers. When W. Greening of the 90th Regiment read it on an armoured train, as he tells in his diary on 1st January 1900, it had become,

> "Hold the train for I am coming
> Buller signals still.
> Wave the answer back to Kruger
> We mean to take the hill."

The *Ladysmith Lyre's* comment on the situation was that 'The Second Army Corps has been discovered in the pigeon holes of the War Office'.

After Platrand the siege took a different turn. Both sides seemed to think that survival was the object in view. This was understandable on the part of those within the pale, but those beyond too seem to have had the stuffing knocked out of them. Of course, they had good days like those after the victory of Spion Kop, but they now settled for containment, their commanders struggling to keep as many men from going home as they could.

For those in town, the tangible enemies were the shelling, starvation and sickness. Enteric was now having a field day.

On the 16 January, Sergeant-Major Shaw wrote,

'The sickness here is terrible and on the increase, we have no less than 1,700 men in hospital on this date, and if the relief column do [sic] not soon arrive I am afraid this number will be increased as they cannot get the necessary medical comforts for the poor fellows. I am keeping in good health myself, although 50 per cent of my men are sick.'

Shaw's concern is creditable in a war when many of the British Commanders showed callous disregard for their men. The wounded that ended up in hospital were in a sad state indeed.

On 17 January, Nevinson of the *Daily Chronicle* claimed that 32 premature births had occurred thanks to the shelling. Of the original 13,500 [his figure] men, only 9,500 were now fit for duty, and the coal used to heat the drinking water condensers had run out.

On the 23rd the British stirred themselves, though when we consider the dwindling ammunition, it was more of a stretch than a fit.

Rawlinson was credited with the idea of the great barrage that commenced early that morning with all sectors of the British defences firing away. The objective, it appeared, was to attempt to find out how many Boers were present and to divert their attention from Buller's pressure. At least one officer recorded his scorn of the plan, remarking on the gross waste of ammunition. This same officer was also critical of the preparation of a food convoy for Buller's troops, which he saw as being at Ladysmith's expense.

The next day gave the defenders even greater reason to question their superiors, in private of course, for the battle of Spion Kop was witnessed from the town, and on the 25th a large body of British soldiers was seen marching by, in step, to captivity.

By January 27 there were 1314 cases of fever or dysentery at Intombi with eight a day dying.

Private J. Clarke of the Manchesters noted in his diary on 28 January that this was the last day of the bread ration and that there was no more grain for the horses. He must have been in the know, for on 1 February a large number of horses were shot, as feed had run out and they were worn out.

They still had some value, though and the knacker's work was not to supply the glue trade, but the 'Chevril' factory at the station. The engine shed was partly adapted as a meat factory, where, under the

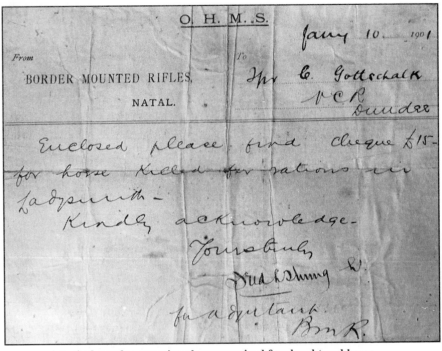

A typical voucher covering cheque received for slaughtered horse.
COURTESY OF NATAL WITNESS

direction of Lieutenant McNalty of the Army Service Corps, the carcasses were boiled down to make soup. According to Nevinson of the *Daily Chronicle* one British soldier remarked, 'Mind that stuff, it kicks!' as he carried it away.

A source wrote that there were actually five products produced at the 'factory.'

1. The soup, Chevril.
2. A condensed version for hospital use.
3. Jelly, similar to calf's foot.
4. The meat itself, very like Potted Meat.
5. 'Neat's-foot oil', used to lubricate the heavy naval guns.

At this time H. H. S. Pearce, the Daily News' Special Correspondent wrote,

'it has come at last. Horseflesh is to be served out for food, instead of being buried or cremated. We do not take it in solid form yet, or at least not consciously, but Colonel Ward has set up a factory with Lieutenant McNalty as managing director [sic], for the conversion of horseflesh into extract of meat under the inviting name of Chevril.'

Dwelling on the subject may disgust some readers, but empty bellies make the best sauce, and here again the soldiers could make the best of a bad job with a bad pun - 'Chevril' being a derivative of 'Bovril'.

Of course, those better paid, or just, in the case of civilians, better off, fared better; and there is a larder of evidence of a lively market in luxuries as well as previously mundane foods like potatoes and eggs, now exotic in themselves. On the 2nd, General White told his diary that a dozen bottles of whisky had changed hands at £12. 5. 0.

The deterioration in the quality of the soldiers' rations is highlighted in these remarks addressed to the diary of Private Arthur Nicholls. Back in November, on Thursday 2nd he had written,

'We were under arms by 4.15am and marched under the hill between Cove Redoubt and Gordon's Post to guard and cover the big guns.

Our Sailor lads opened fire on Long Tom at about 5 am and three shots were fired before they answered by several shots but doing little damage. We marched to camp for breakfast at 7.45. As soon as we got in we found the enemy was shelling the camp. Our breakfast consisted of coffee, bread, butter, jam and a few shells from the enemy but they have done no damage.'

There are worse breakfasts than that but, on 5 February, the day, by coincidence, that Horse Sausage was issued for the first time, Private Nicholls wrote,

'The night went on but there was no attack. We was [sic] relieved about 5am the 5th. We had chevril made out of horseflesh for breakfast. The meat it is made from they will give away to anyone who will fetch it. Troops can be seen bringing in their handkerchief full all the day. I had some myself and I liked it very much. Many a gentleman's son can be seen getting it from them and they all say they like it, anything so long as it fills up.'

On 8 February, Shaw added to his report,

'We have now reached the 100th day of the siege, and still no relief, it is getting rather serious, consequently our rations have been reduced. We get now 8oz of biscuit or bread and 3/4 lb. of horse flesh, 1/6th of an ounce of tea and 1 oz. of sugar per diem, not a very large quantity to keep a man going. We had four of the finest cavalry regiments in the army with us, but we are having to kill their horses for food, and the men do outpost duty to replace casualties in the infantry. I can assure you we know what it is to be hungry, as the amount of food is scarcely sufficient to keep us going. Articles of food have reached an enormous price in Ladysmith, for instance, condensed milk, 6/- a tin; a 1/4lb cake of hard tobacco, 15/-; small bunch of carrots, 7/6; matches 1/- a box; 1 gall. of potatoes, 24/-; eggs, 37/6 a doz.; sugar 1/- a lb; brandy, £5 for a bottle; and other articles proportionately dear; these are now unobtainable.'

Leicesters with Maxim.

He does not mention it, but presumably, he heard the rumour abroad that Mafeking had been relieved.

On 9 February, Pearse agreed that things were bad, but said with a bit more style.

'We are now down to one pound of meat, including horse, 4 ounces of mealie meal, 4 ounces of bread, with a sausage ration daily, as far as possible. Sausages may be mysteries elsewhere, but we know them here to be horseflesh, highly spiced, and nothing more. Bread is a brown, 'clitty' mixture of mealie meal, starch and the unknown. Vegetables we have none, except a so called wild spinach that overgrew every neglected garden and

Boer Dam on the Klip River, repeatedly breached by artillery fire.
COURTESY OF NATAL WITNESS

could be had for the taking until people discovered how precious it was.'

One wonders how the Zulu and other non-European inhabitants were faring by now. Maybe it was as in Mafeking, where deaths from starvation or malnutrition related sickness were commonplace; S. T. Plaatje, the first Secretary of the African National Congress, was there at the time as a court interpreter. He was an educated and sensitive man

with a somewhat pompous writing style, and his life was dedicated to disappointment. He is valuable as a commentator in that he was black, educated, and saw it all.

His Diary says on this point,

> 'it was a miserable scene to be surrounded by about 50 hungry beings, agitating the engagement of your pity and to see one of them succumb to his agonies and fall backwards with a dead thud.'

It would be interesting to read the diary of an African in the Siege of Ladysmith too.

On the 10th Pearse wrote on another popular theme:

> 'Depression sets in again, and, as always happens when there is bad news or dread of it, the death rate at Intombi Hospital Camp has gone up to 15 in a single day.'

The Boers were failing to read the effects of their hundred-day surveillance. Instead of testing the amount of ammunition that the British had left and then attacking them again, they were content to try to dam Klip River below Ntombi by filling it with sandbags - while the sailors' long 12s and 42nd Battery's 15 pounders blasted them away again. Almost more important, as well as completely irrelevant to most, was a record that eggs had reached 52/- a dozen.

If Tommy Atkins could not pay over 4/- for an egg he was, at least, 'egged on' by news from the real world. On the 16th the fall of Kimberley was known. It served to further spice the horse-sausage and to encourage the soldiers to last out, but the men were becoming weaker and weaker. Private J. Clarke of the Manchesters records the following siege prices.

2 plates of grapes	£2. 6. 0.
1 doz. eggs	£2. 8. 0.
Vegetable Marrow	£1. 7. 6.
1 packet of cigs (usually 3d.)	£1. 5. 0.
Tin of jam (usually 6d.)	£1. 3. 0.
Bottle of home-made jam	£1. 11. 6.
Box of Sunlight Soap (usually 9d.)	18. 0.

At Christmas, two months before, jam had been recorded at 3/6 per lb., eggs at half a guinea a dozen and whisky at £5 to £7 per bottle.

By comparison, the cost of living in England included tea at 2/- per lb, suits made to measure at 35/-, ham at 7d per lb, XXXX Beer at 1/6 a gallon and the rent of a house at 4/- a week. An unmarried soldier's pay was 1/- a day.

A hopeful sight on 19 February was of 171 Boer wagons plodding northwards with many men, but no one could be sure when the end would come and by the 25th eggs reached 5/- apiece and two pennorth of tobacco in a cake fetched 19/6d.

Captain Edmund (Ted) Fisher of the 1/Manchesters was, after the war, the model for the official Regimental War Memorial in St. Ann's Square, Manchester. This was the work of Mr. Hamo Thorneycroft, and was unveiled in the presence of Sir Ian Hamilton on the 26th October

Boer Prisoners in Ladysmith. COURTESY OF NATAL WITNESS

1908 - the year before Captain Fisher died. The statue is that of a soldier at the ready, with fixed bayonet, being offered a round by a wounded man at his feet.

The author learned of this officer's presence in the siege from his nephew, Mr Reggie Fair, and Captain Fisher's grandson Mr. Mark Walford kindly gave the author sight of the captain's letter to a friend in England dated March 13 1900. It is a jolly and optimistic piece, in spite of the rigours of the past four months, and the rest that Buller allowed after his victory benefited the half-starved garrison and Buller's ragged, dirty Relief Column alike.

> 'There doesn't seem to be any news. We hardly realize that it is still war-time. We move from here to Dewdrop on Friday, about 9 miles away, I believe. I don't know how the men will manage such a long walk though they have improved wonderfully since the relief. Before it, they were quite painfully weak in addition to lack of boots.'

In view of the honours heaped upon White and the congratulations thrown about among the various members and political friends of Lord Robert's Ring, Captain Fisher's postscript is both clipped and interesting.

'Sir G. White seems to be the hero of the hour. Why?'

On the 23rd the shelling of the dam was still going on, as Pearse wrote,

'For several days past the Naval 12-pounders on Caesar's Camp have shelled the Boers at work on the dam below Intombi Camp causing much consternation. One result of this is that Bulwaan (the 155mm Creusot on Umbulwana) tries to keep down the 12-pounders' fire and leaves the town in comparative quiet.'

Suddenly things brightened up. On the 28th Pearse observed,

'Few of us, however, were prepared for the sight that met our eyes as we looked from Observation Hill across the broad plain towards Blaauwbank when the mists of morning cleared. There we saw Boer convoys trekking northwards from the Tugela past Spion Kop in columns miles long. Others emerged from the defile by Underbrook like huge serpents twining about the hillsides. Wagons were crowded together by hundreds.... Bulwaan fired a single shot by way of a parting salute, and then a tripod was rigged up for lifting 'Puffing Billy' from his carriage. It was a bold thing to do in broad daylight, and our Naval 12-pounders made short work of it by battering the tripod over.'

The Siege was over and, like Waterloo, it was a close-run thing. On March 1st, Pearse sent someone a telegram noting that there were only 4 days rations left when the siege ended, with 800 sick and wounded in Intombi.

The Hospital Statistics, as published in the Official History, make interesting reading, showing 600 deaths. 510 of these were from enteric or dysentery and only 59 from wounds.

On 4 November, there were 12 cases of dysentery in hospital and no cases of enteric. Two weeks later there were two patients of enteric along with 21 of dysentery, but as the numbers steadily climbed, the number of those suffering from enteric overtook that of those with

The ragged Relief Force parades, guarded by the half starved garrison.

dysentery. In week of January 27th, when the hospital was at its busiest, there were 842 patients on hand with the fever and 472 with dysentery. This was the peak, but even when the relief force arrived, the sick there still numbered 708 and 341.

According to the Official History the expenditure of ammunition amounted to 514 shells by the 4.7s, 784 from the Naval 12-pounders, 776 howitzer shells, 3768 shells from 15-pounders, and 25 shells from 9-pounders. Then there were 101 rounds from 2.5", 48 from Maxims, 80 Hotchkiss and 213.400 Lee Metford rounds, over half of which were in the Platrand battle.

The Blessed Day had now arrived and the rewards and retributions would begin. First, however, was the strange spectacle of the official entry of the Relief Force when the parade was of fit men, though dirty and in rags - and the guard of honour, lining the streets, was of weak starvelings.

There was still the small matter of clearing the invaders out of Natal, but for those who had been besieged the particular uncertainty was over, giving place to new imponderables.

At least there was medical help and sufficient food. The railway was open and the road clear, so that essential humanitarian activities could proceed.

For the Relief Force, there was a rest and then the pursuit out of Natal of the Boer Army, and for the latter, the descent into guerrilla warfare, defeat, and ultimate success at the founding of the Union of South Africa.

Soldiers did not know that they were preparing for World War 1, but inevitably, they were. Of course, many men of all ranks ended their service before the Great War began, but particularly among the senior career officers, who depended less on physical condition, and more, you would suppose, on organising and inspirational skills, there was great fame or high notoriety waiting.

Captain Edmund Fisher's health must have suffered in his time in South Africa, for he died in 1909.

General Sir George White VC, whose worth as a commander was in doubt in the mind of at least one of his officers, as well as in his own, was rewarded with the Governorship of Gibraltar, staying until 1905, and a Field Marshall's baton in 1903. He died in 1912.

Sir Archibald Hunter, his Chief of Staff, who had commanded a Division at Omdurman, when he was highly thought of by Kitchener, was given command of 10th Division, as a Lieutenant General. He became a General in 1905 and spent the Great War, up to 1917,

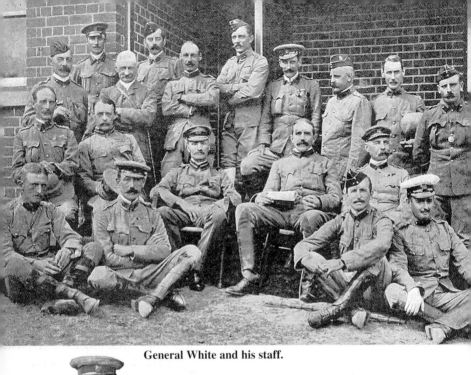

General White and his staff.

training the New Armies. He retired in 1920.

Henry Rawlinson, who is said to have suggested that Naval Guns be brought up, and who lost his chair, became a General in January 1917, after his great idea for the Somme had cost so many lives. His association with the casualty lists of July 1st 1916 did him no harm and in 1918, he presided over the greatest British advance of the war. He was appointed C in C in India in 1920, dying in Delhi in 1925.

Ian Hamilton had a 'good' Boer War and by 1907 was a full General. He was in charge at the Dardanelles in 1915 until recalled. He died as recently as 1947.

Captain Hedworth Lambton's career prospered as far as Commander in Chief of the China Station between 1908 and 1910. In 1911 he changed his name to Meux and was MP for Portsmouth from 1916 to 1918. He died in 1925.

Percy Scott's vigour never dimmed and he retired in 1913 as an Admiral and a Baronet. In 1915-1916 he was in charge of London's gunnery defences against aircraft. He ended his days in 1920.

General Yule, who brought the Dundee garrison home

Sir Henry Rawlinson.

to Ladysmith, faded from the story and was awarded the CB in 1900, dying in 1920 as Colonel Yule.

Cecil William Park, that gentleman who stood in the crackling Mauser fire with Hamilton on Wagon Hill, became ADC to the King and was a Major-General when he died in 1913.

Young Lieutenant Halsey went on to several engagements in the Great War, rising to be an Admiral and to command the Royal Australian Navy. After this, he was Comptroller and Treasurer to Prince of Wales from 1920 to 1936. He died in 1949.

Private Scott VC went on to become Regimental Quartermaster Sergeant, dying in 1961. His colleague Private Pitts made Lance Corporal before he left the service and he died in 1955.

Sergeant Talbot went on with his 42nd Battery through the Transvaal and, when the war was over, continued his career. In April 1908, for instance, he was awarded a Gunnery Certificate for his part in a Short Field Course.

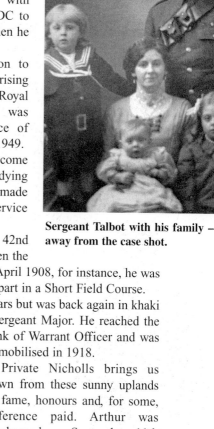

Sergeant Talbot with his family – away from the case shot.

He left the army in 1911 after 23 years but was back again in khaki in 1918, going to France as Battery Sergeant Major. He reached the rank of Warrant Officer and was demobilised in 1918.

Private Nicholls brings us down from these sunny uplands of fame, honours and, for some, deference paid. Arthur was discharged on September 11th 1902 with ten years' service, typical of the enlisted man. Having 'done his bit', he went home to honest obscurity until his diary was discovered in 1991.

The show was over and the spotlight on Ladysmith went out.

Boer War Memorial, Manchester, modelled by Captain E. Fisher.

Boer War Memorial, York.

INDEX

Adelaide Farm 46

Albrecht, Major R. Orange Free State
Artillery. 29

Albrecht VC, Trooper H., Imperial
Light Horse (*posthumous*)
80,117,123

Ava, Lieutenant Lord. 17/ Lancers 115,
116, 121

Baden Powell, Colonel R.S.S. 75

Bell's Kop 75, 92

Bester's Farm, Valley 109, 111

Biggarsberg Mountains 32, 34, 53

Boer Memorial, Platrand 125

Boseley, Sergeant 114

Botha, General Louis 30,107

Brabant, Lieutenant A. E., Imperial
Light Horse 62

British Imperial and Irregular Units -
Bethune's Mounted Infantry 55
Border Mounted Rifles 74, 94
Imperial Light Horse 54, 55, 58, 59,
60, 61, 62, 64, 67, 74, 80, 91, 92,
101, 107, 110, 114, 115, 119, 120, 122
Natal Carbineers 32, 74, 101
Natal Police 32, 74
Natal Mounted Rifles 58, 74
Natal Naval Volunteers 74, 110
South African Light Horse 55
Thorneycroft's Mounted Infantry 55

British Units-
5/Dragoon Guards 57, 58, 62, 73, 78, 80
18/Hussars 32, 40, 74, 84,114, 123
19/Hussars 67, 73, 101, 114
5/Lancers 54, 57, 58, 59, 62, 67, 73,
92, 114
1/Devonshire Regiment 57, 59, 61,
62, 67, 73, 78, 80, 83, 103, 118,
119, 120, 121
2/Dublin Fusiliers 32, 39, 41, 42, 74,
75, 81, 87
1/Gloucestershire Regiment 67, 68,
74, 81, 83

2/Gordon Highlanders 57, 58, 59, 60,
62, 64, 74, 80, 81, 94, 95,103,110,
111, 114, 115, 118

1/ Kings Royal Rifle Corps 32, 41,
42, 44, 74, 78

2/ Kings Royal Rifle Corps 67, 73,
78, 81,107,111,114, 115, 116, 118

1/Leicestershire Regiment 32, 41, 65,
74, 77, 83, 85, 130

1/Liverpool Regiment 67, 73, 74, 78,
81, 83, 87, 94,101, 114

1/Manchester Regiment 55, 59, 60,
73, 80, 81, 92, 107, 109, 111, 112,
113, 114, 118, 119, 123, 127, 134

2/Rifle Brigade 74, 113, 114, 123

Royal Engineers 55, 74, 80,101,122

1/Royal Irish Fusiliers 32, 41, 42, 43,
74, 81, 83, 84, 106

York and Lancaster Regiment 16

10th Mountain Battery 67, 73, 81,
83, 84

13th Battery RFA 32, 42, 74

21st Battery RFA 57, 59, 73, 115

42nd Battery RFA 17, 57, 58, 59, 67,
73, 92, 110, 113, 118, 133, 139

53rd Battery RFA 67,73,113,114

67th Battery RFA 32, 33, 41, 74

69th Battery RFA 32, 42, 74

Naval Brigade 73, 74, 75, 85,135

Brocklehurst, Major-General J. F. 90

Buller, General Sir Redvers 26, 80, 96,
97,118, 127, 135

Butler, Lieutenant General Sir W. F. 20

Caesar's Camp 75, 78, 88, 92, 107, 109,
111, 113, 114, 115, 116, 118, 122,
124, 125

Cardwell, Edward 15

Carleton, Lieutenant-Colonel F.R.C.,
1/Irish Fusiliers 81, 83, 84

Carnegie, Captain the Hon R. F.
2/Gordon Highlanders 111,113,114

Chamberlain, Sir Joseph. British
Colonial Secretary 22, 23, 24

Chevril 78,127,128,129

Colenso 20, 59, 76, 95

Cove Redoubt 78, 88, 89, 96, 114

141

Craw, Bella - Diarist 80,

Creusot 155mm Guns 21, 31, 50, 65, 69, 79, 85, 95, 99, 105,106, 114, 135

Cronje, General Piet 30

Curran, Lieutenant-Colonel, 1/Mancesters 60, 111, 113, 114

Darbyshire, Captain P.H. 5/Dragoon Guards 57

Dartnell, Colonel J. G. 68

Davies, Major Walter 'Karri' 54, 55, 79, 101, 103, 117

De Jager, Field Cornet Zacharius 116, 117

De Villiers, Boer General C.J. 107,116,120

De Villiers, Field-Cornet Japie 116,117,122

Denne, Major H.W.D. 1/Gordon Highlanders 59, 61

Dennis, Lieutenant G. B. B. RE 117

Dick Cunyngham, Lieutenant-Colonel W.H. 57, 60, 80, 91, 99, 102, 104, 111, 112

Digby-Jones VC, R.J.T., Lieutenant. Royal Engineers (posthumous) 80, 110, 116, 117, 122, 123

Dragoon Guards Monument 78, 106

Drakensberg 33, 53

Dundee 10,35,36, 44, 45,46,51,67,69,72,75

Egerton, F. G. Commander RN 88, 89

Elandslaagte 33,51,56,58,60,67,68,91,101

Erasmus, 'Maroola'. General 33, 35, 41

Field, Lieutenant, 1/Devonshires 119, 120, 121

Fiddling Jimmy 79

Fisher, Captain Edmund 1/Manchesters 134, 135, 137, 139

Fitzpatrick, Percy 55

Flynne,Private 2/Dublin Fusiliers 45

HMS *Forte* 99,102

French, Major-General J. D. P. 54, 55, 57, 58, 61, 67, 81

Frazer, Private (the Fenian) 59

Ghandi, M. K. 95, 96

Glencoe 48, 51, 66, 69

Gordon Hill 75, 78, 88, 89, 96, 114

Gore-Brown, Major H. 2/KRRC 107,111

Gorman, Private 5078 1/Dublin Fusiliers 44

Gough, Captain John 2/Rifle Brigade 80,113

Gough, Captain Hubert 16/Lancers 80

Grimwood, Colonel G. G. 81

Gun Hill 75,101

Gunning, Lieutenant Colonel R. H. 1/KRRC 44, 46

Guthrie-Smith, Trooper, Imperial Light Horse 91

Haggard, Sir Henry Rider 35

Halsey, Liuetenant RN 139

Hambro, Lieutenant N. J. 1/KRRC 44

Hamilton, Colonel Ian S. M. 57,58,59,60, 61,64,67,77,8,81,111,115,116,117,118, 119, 121, 124, 134, 138, 139

Hannah, Lieutenant W.M.J., 1/Leicestershires 49, 65

Harris, Rear Admiral Sir Robert 79

Hart, Lieutenant General A. Fitzroy 59

Helpmekaar 36, 81

Helpmekaar Ridge, Ladysmith 75,78,92

Hely-Hutchinson, Sir Walter 32

Hodges, Michael, Lieutenant RN 88

Howard, General F. 78,102

Howitzers 'Castor and Pollux'. 78, 79,106

Hunt-Grubbe, Lieutenant R., 1/Manchesters 113, 123, 125

Hunter, Major-General Sir Archibald 32, 75, 80, 85, 86, 87, 101, 103, 137

Impati 36, 41, 46, 50, 65

Indumeni 36, 37

Intintanyoni 67

Intombi Camp and Hospital 91,104,114, 133, 135,136

Irish Brigade 59

Jameson, Dr. Leander Starr 22, 79

Jameson Raid 19, 22, 55, 79

Jones, Captain E. P., RN. 99

Jonono's Kop 57, 67

Johnstone VC, Captain R., Imperial Light Horse 62

Junction Hill 75, 88

Joubert, Commandant-General Piet 14,16, 30, 31, 33, 35, 50, 53, 65, 78, 84, 90,125

Joubert, Mrs. 114

Kestell, Pastor J. D. 122

Kimberley 78, 10, 133

King's Post 75, 76, 78

Klip River 71, 74, 75, 78, 94, 110,132,133

Knox, Major E. C. 18/Hussars 46

Knox, Colonel W. G. - 'Nasty Knox' 78, 87

Kok, General J. H. M. 31, 35, 51, 57, 53, 60, 61, 63

Kruger Paul, President, South African Republic 14,15,16,19, 20, 23, 24, 25

Lady Anne Battery 78, 88, 110

Ladysmith, Natal 51, 54, 64, 68, 69, 70, 71, 74, 75, 76, 78, 90, 91, 94, 106

Ladysmith Bombshell 98

Ladysmith Lyre 24, 96, 97, 99, 126

Ladysmith Siege Museum 20, 72, 76, 77, 94, 101, 106, 117

Lafone, Captain 1/Devonshires 119,120,121

Lambton RN, Captain the Hon.Hedworth 75, 85, 87, 91, 114, 138

Lansdowne, Marquis of British War Minister 24, 25

Lawrence, Drum Major 2/Gordon Highlanders 60

Leicester Memorial 77, 78, 106

Lennox Hill 36, 40, 41, 42, 44

Limit Hill 75, 85, 101

Lombard's Kop 75, 81, 83, 94

Long Hill 81,101

Long Tom 65, 79, 88, 94, 101, 106, 129

Mafeking 75, 78,131, 132

Magersfontein 20

Majuba Hill, *Amajuba* 17, 25, 64, 107, 117

Manchester Fort, Caesar's Camp 109, 110, 111, 122, 123

Manchester Regiment's War Memorial 64, 124, 134, 139

Masterson VC, Lieutenant J. E. I., 1/Devonshires 80, 119, 120, 121, 123

Matthias, Captain, Imperial Light Horse 110, 111, 115

Maud, W.T., reporter of the Graphic 79

McMasters' Blockhouse 77

Meiklejohn VC, Captain M.F.M., 1/Gordon Highlanders 61

Metcalf, Lietenant Colonel C. T. E,. 2/Rifle Brigde 114

Meyer, Boer General Lukas 10, 31, 39, 41, 48, 53

Miller-Walnutt, Major C. C. 2/Gordon Highlanders 115, 116, 117

Milner, Sir Alfred. British High Commissioner 20, 22, 23, 24

Mkupe's Pass 35, 53, 57

Modder River 20

Modder Spruit 54, 57, 58, 81, 101

Moller, Lieutenant Colonel B. D. 18/ Hussars 40, 41, 46, 48, 84

Mournful Monday - 30th October 69, 72

Mullins CMG, VC, Major C.H. 55, 62

Murray, Lord George 59

Nevinson, reporter of the *Daily Chronicle* 63, 79, 80, 127, 128

Newcastle 33, 35, 50, 57

Nicholson's Nek 78, 83, 87, 91

Nicholls, Private Arthur, 1/Leicesters 85, 129, 139

Norwood VC, Lieutenant J., 5/Dragoon Guards 80, 83

Observation Hill 75, 77, 78, 107, 135

Orange River Sovereignty, Transorangia 13

Parbhusingh, Mr. 95

Park, Lieutenant-Colonel C. W. 1/Devonshires 57,80,118,119,120,121,139

Pearse, H.H.S., reporter of the '*Daily Chronicle*' 80, 131, 133, 135, 136

Pechell, Captain M. H. K., 1/KRRC 44, 46

Pepworth Hill 69, 75, 79, 85

Pitts VC, Private James, 1/Manchesters 80,123,124,139

Plaatje, Solomon Tshekisho 132

Prinsloo, Marthinius. Chief Commandant 31, 35, 53

Platrand 68, 75, 107, 108, 110, 126

16, Poort Road. White's HQ 92, 93, 103

HMS *Powerful* 103, 110

Puffing Billy 79, 92, 95, 103, 114, 136

Range Post 75, 77, 115

Ration Post 75

Rawlinson, Sir Henry 79, 80, 92, 103, 127, 138

Reservoir Hill 78

143

Rietfontein 67, 81, 91
Rifleman's Ridge 75, 77, 114
1895 Reform Committee 55, 60
Rhodes, Colonel Frank 55, 79, 103, 115
Rhodes, Cecil John 18, 19
Robertson VC, Sergeant-Major W.
1/Gordon Highlanders 61
Royal Hotel 76, 94
Sand River Convention 13
Schalk Burger, Boer General 107, 125
Schiel, Colonel 51, 57, 58, 60
Scott, Captain Percy RN 75, 79, 84, 88,
    102, 138
Scott VC, Private Robert, 1/Manchesters
    80, 123, 124, 139
Scott-Chisholme, Colonel J. J. 54, 61, 64, 65
Shaw, Sergeant-Major Walter 80, 94,
    102, 127, 129
Sherston, Colonel J. DSO 2/Rifle
Brigade., 44, 46
Signpost Hill 75, 115
Sims, Gunner W., RN 110, 116, 117
Smith, Sir Harry 12, 70
Smith, Lady 71
Smith's Farm 35, 36, 37, 41
Smith's Nek 42, 44, 46
Spion Kop 55, 76, 77, 96, 103, 117, 126, 127
Star Hill 75
Stark, Dr A. C. 92, 94
Steevens, George. reporter of the
    Daily Mail 79
Streatfield, Captain Eric, 1/Gordon
    Highlanders 60, 61
Steavenson, Captain, Mounted Infantry
    1/Liverpools 80, 87
Surprise Hill 75, 78, 102
Symons, Major-General Sir W. Penn
    24, 31, 32, 39, 40, 41, 42, 43, 48, 49,
    50, 66, 75
Talana Hill 31, 34, 36, 39, 41, 44, 47, 119
Talbot, Sergeant F. E., 42nd Battery RFA
    17, 96, 113, 139
HMS Tartar 99
Taylor, Lieutenant. 1/KRRC 44
Telegraph Ridge 75, 79, 125
HMS Terrible 79, 99, 103

Tchrengula 78
Tin Camp 74, 80
Tugela, Heights of 20
Tugela River 75
Umbulwana 75, 79, 91, 94, 104, 114, 135
Van Riebeeck, Jan Van 11
Van Tonder's Nek 66
de Villebois-Mareuil, Colonel Compte
    29, 37
Viljoen, Boer General Ben 31
Wagon Hill 75, 107, 110, 111, 114, 115,
    116, 118, 121, 122, 125,
Walker, Lieutenant. Somerset Light
    Infantry 119, 120, 121
Waschbank 66, 67
Weldon, Captain G.A.1/Dublin Fusiliers 44
Wessels, Gert 116, 117
White, General Sir George Stewart 17,
    31,39,54,57,67,75,79,80,89,92,93,
        103,111,114,118,129,135,137,138
Wilford, Lieutenant Colonel E. P.,
    1/Gloucesters 68
Wolmarans, J. F. Major. Transvaal State
    Artillery 40
Wools-Sampson, Lieutenant-Colonel A.
    54, 55, 79
Yule, Colonel J.H. 41, 42, 65, 66, 67, 68,
    69, 120, 138